THERE COMES

a LIGHT:

A Memoir of Mental Illness

By

Elaina J. Martin

Barking Dog Press
5110 Utile Rd.
Fayetteville, NC 28304

Author: Elaina J. Martin
Copyeditor: Jenna Bagnini
Cover Design: S. Dassanayake
Interior Design: Winnie G. O.
Front Cover Photography: Jennifer Wilson
Back Cover Photography: Sharon Martin

There Comes a Light: A Memoir of Mental Illness/ Elaina J.
Martin.
ISBN: 978-1-7320073-4-5

I dedicate this memoir to my mom, without whom I would not be here to tell this tale. I couldn't live this life without you, Mom. Thank you a million times over. XOXO

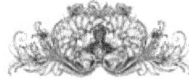

CHAPTER 1

Blog post

September 13, 2007

You know I'm a big fan of reinvention. My whole life I've lived as though I'm a gypsy. I don't know how to stay in one place. And so, once again, I am on the move. My bags are being packed, my oil changed, my maps laid out.

It's scary, you know? Just because I do it willingly doesn't mean I'm not scared, but life's too short to wait it out.

My row to hoe's been tough lately. There are tangles of weeds and rocks the size of lemons. But I just keep working at it, cultivating it. The soil is rich; I just need to clear it. Some of you have watched me struggle, offering help, but knowing it is my row, I must manage it myself.

Waiting

The tubes in the intensive care unit at San Mateo Hospital in California enter my body at various spots—mouth and arms. Eyes closed, I dream, or perhaps it is only darkness I see. The blue gown thin as a sheet of paper spun from cotton covers me. My curly hair is spread across the pillow that cannot be plumped, and when you walk into the room you might think I am merely sleeping. Beside me sits a scared young woman, her face much like mine: my baby sister, Angela. Her emerald eyes watch my chest—up and down, up and down—afraid that if she looks away, even for a moment, the movement might cease. It is October 2nd, 2007, and I've had an accident.

Accidentally on purpose I've tried to kill myself.

I had woken up the day of my suicide attempt oblivious to the fact, to the idea, that in the course of the next twenty-four hours I would try to take my life. Instead, I busied myself preparing for the fourth day of my new job. As a style editor of an up-and-coming website I felt like I had finally found a job where I could focus solely on my passion. I had a bachelor's degree in apparel design and had spent years assisting fashion editors, working on runway shows during Fashion Week, styling photo shoots in New York, and eventually editing magazines in Austin, Texas.

With my experience to back me up, I was in the cozy town of San Mateo just outside of San Francisco, with a title I had long sought. During the day I wrote about designers and styles and became an authority on all things fashionable. My coworkers were friendly. I liked my assistant. Things were on an upswing. The day came to an end with beers all around as we prepared to watch the vice-presidential debate. Back home my roommate, Abigail, and I relaxed with cigarettes out on our patio. We were at the top of the stairs on the second floor overlooking the pool. If you turned right at the top of the steps, you were at the apartment belonging to the cute guys across the way. If you turned left, you were home. We didn't have a television, so we watched the debate on Abigail's laptop, each holding a tumbler of wine in hand.

After the debate I took my second glass of red down to the pool and sat with my toes dangling under the surface. It had grown dark and the air hung warm around me; the water glowed a luminous aqua. I called my cousin, Kimberly, in Oklahoma and we dissected my new gig, missing each other already. We talked excitedly about the idea of her attending law school at Stanford and the two of us marrying intelligent grads of the university. I recall feeling wildly happy. Sometime after the call ended, I wrote a note. A suicide note. I don't remember what I said. I sent a text message to my boss telling him I was feeling under the weather—a stomach ache of some sort—and was unsure if I would be at work the following day.

Then I swallowed all the tiny peach Xanax pills—a medication prescribed for my anxiety and obsessive compulsive disorder—that were inside the orange bottle. After ingesting the fistfuls of pills in a few gulps I waited, wondering if I would come to the realization that I had made a mistake. I didn't. At peace I lay down in my new bed, knowing I would never wake up again and that that was okay. That was right. I was ready to die.

I don't know what happened, what overtook me in those moments. It was as though someone other than me was in charge of my mind, my hands, my mouth. I was not depressed. On the contrary, I was where I believed I should be, in a job I was falling in love with. They say stress can lead to psychotic breaks—when you lose touch with reality for a while. Before I swallowed all those pills, everything had been new to me—my job, my apartment, my roommate, my city; the very air I breathed was different and my stress level was at its peak.

I'm not sure what made me decide to try to take my life that particular night. I only know what was told to me and what I remembered days later. Around midnight the night of the attempt my roommate went to the kitchen for a glass of water and found me unconscious on the floor. I must have gone in there for some water for myself before hitting the linoleum. She couldn't wake me so she called my sister in San Francisco, a short drive away, and my sister dropped everything and rushed to the apartment. Before Angela arrived, my roommate found the suicide note and called 911. An ambulance came for me, lights flashing, alarms blaring, We must save someone. We must be fast. Hurry. Hurry. They took me to San Mateo Hospital's emergency room. Stomach pumped, intubated, IVs inserted into my tan skin. Watching.

Waiting. My parents flew in from Oklahoma, no jet fast enough to get them to their baby girl, no ticket price too high.

"She might not wake up. She may have brain damage. She may die," the doctors said, in sobering heavy words. "We must wait and see."

I woke in intensive care; bits of my surroundings remain in my memory like sunlight filtering through the ocean's surface. My sister sat on the left side of my hospital bed. It was her birthday. I couldn't speak to her with a tube down my throat and words were lost in my mind. The feeling of the tubes being pulled from my body is the only other memory I have of my ICU stay. "Cough," said the nurse, as they pulled the breathing tube up my throat. And that is all.

I opened my eyes and we were making pizza. Someone told me to put pepperoni on the pie in front of me. I knew no one, yet I knew them all. I walked out into a larger room half-filled with wooden tables; beyond the nurses' desk, soft, upholstered maroon-patterned chairs took up more space than they needed. Minutes later my parents pushed through the double hospital doors, followed by my sister. I was so relieved to see them because I wasn't quite sure where I was or what I was doing there. I hugged each of them, holding them tightly, not wanting to let go. I asked them to explain and we sat talking about things I would never remember; things I would forget as soon as they were said. It was hard to find the right words; my dictionary was gone. An hour had passed when they stood to leave. To leave me behind. Two days I had been in the psychiatric ward at Hope Mills Peninsula Hospital. Again, those days are lost in the sea of sadness that slammed into me like a tidal wave upon my waking in the ICU. The rules of the ward had been explained to me during the two days I had been in, so when I became more conscious of my surroundings I knew them, like waking into a childhood home I had all but forgotten—familiar yet foreign and strange.

I shared a room just big enough for two twin beds, two

chairs, and a chest of drawers with a woman I took to calling Dora the Explorer. I don't know why. She was ancient, in her 90s. Her name was Anna. Once she had taught art at New York University; a notable artist. She had been someone. She had been important. Now she was holding on to the railing, shuffling down the hallway in her faded hospital gown. Lost. One afternoon I came in to find her quietly sobbing in her bed, a sound of sorrow so overwhelming I hear it still. She did not speak to me, only lay there remembering what once was her life. During my stay I did what I could to help the old lady, steadying her down the hall for her medication, calling her to breakfast, listening when she spoke. She told me she was waiting for a facility to open up, to keep her the rest of her days. Waiting.

Each day we rose for a meal we had chosen from a paper menu the day before—circling our decisions in advance, learning to hang on until tomorrow for corn flakes or cold toast. Our decaffeinated coffee came to our table in small Styrofoam cups on a plastic tray, our plasticware kept us safe, and sugar never snuck into our food. It was as though they were saying "Avoid the danger, keep them safe, keep them docile—no caffeine, no metal objects, no sugar." After breakfast we lined up in the hall for our turn to stand in front of a door, the top half opened, the bottom closed, like a locked saloon door in an old Western. A nurse handed each of us our particular doses of medications and watched us as though we were small children. She ensured we didn't spit out our pills or hide them under our tongues. It was sedation. It was a secret. I have no idea what I ingested the three times I lined up each day. I followed the rules. I opened my mouth and swallowed.

The morning meetings proved ridiculous; again we were considered without experience—learning to live. The nurse asked us to share the rules of the ward with each other; sometimes a new face among us would absorb them. Volunteers were selected for duties like cleaning the smokers' room or straightening the chairs. "Questions?" Silence. "Go get 'em, tigers."

I chose to attend the movement class following the morning meetings. It wasn't strenuous, just a way to forget where we lived for twenty minutes. We went through a serious of stretches, a far cry from yoga, but it gave me a sense of peace I couldn't find elsewhere inside those walls. Group therapy and occupational therapy were required throughout the day. Therapy. Therapy. We had a break in the day. We had lunch. More pills and potions. And then my favorite part, the short moments I spent with my family. Every day, twice a day, they would come for visiting hours. Never late to arrive, never early to leave, even though I had broken their hearts, even though I could see the pieces floating in their eyes. They couldn't possibly understand why I had done what I had, but they smiled for me. My sister's best friend sent me brownies; my parents snuck in a caffeinated Starbucks Frappucino, insisting to the nurses that there was not a drop of caffeine, of poison, in the plastic cup with the tall green straw. And the flowers, my favorite shade of pale pink, we put in a plastic cup that sat on the floor by my bed. No glass; no danger. They came and they loved me and that was enough.

When locked up there is no air. Not in your room. Not in your lungs. Not through the glass windows. We were kept safe—imprisoned—on a floor in a hospital. We never went out. I would stand by a window at the end of the hall watching construction workers on the other side of the street, longing to feel a hammer in my hand if only to feel the wind on my cheeks. At times I would sit in the great room staring through the sealed window at the hillside dotted with houses. Houses where people lived—normal people—people without suicide notes or hospital gowns, people who were not crazy like us.

The days were long and I did not sleep despite prescriptions to aid me. At night I would sit in the great room gazing at books, reading words I could not see—my vision skewed, my concentration nonexistent. I stared into the deep still dark ocean. There were a few of us; the night dwellers. Scratching the white surface of paper with ferocity. Walking the halls one step carefully measured from the last. Sitting on the floor, head down. Lips moving without sound. And all the while the clock ticked.

Two silver phones hung on the cream walls across from the nurses' station. If they rang, whoever happened to be closest answered and found the man or woman requested. A few calls came for me from friends, family, coworkers, and my old therapist. Some knew where I was and why. My coworkers knew only that I was sick and hospitalized. All asked how I was doing, not sure what to say, awkward words across the miles.

How do you answer that? "I tried to kill myself and am now locked in a psychiatric ward?" "Yes, everything is peachy?" "What the fuck do you think?"

I told each of them I was fine—a truth stretched from a lie that living was better than dying. In the days following my attempt to end my life a depression unlike any other I had experienced sucked me down. Days before I had been buoyant; now I was sinking to the bottom.

I bore no scar from the attempt, nothing physical. My left wrist told its own story. Self-injury. A cry for help. Three inches from my wrist creeping towards my elbow, a purple scar created months prior. Alcohol. Pills. I was obsessed with the idea of taking a blade to my wrist and slicing through the delicate skin to watch it bleed. My mother came to Austin to watch over me. At the doctor's office for a check on my deep gash she was told that had she not been there he would have admitted me to a psych unit.

Inside my new world we were all just treading water, doing our best to keep our heads above the surface. For the first time I could shed my guard, watching it as it sunk beneath the ripples. No more hiding behind a smile, no more rivers of tears in the dark. All of us were broken by no fault of our own. Genetics. Trauma. A life of bad breaks. People understood what it felt like and no one offered trite answers. Regardless of how much I longed to leave the walls, to escape, I felt safe and unashamed of not only the way I understood myself but also the way I saw the world.

I met another young woman. Her wrist looked like mine and she had a five-inch scar to match it along her jaw. Her name was Johanna. To each other we seemed normal. Friends are important when exiled from the world, and she became mine. Feelings no one on the outside could understand we shared without having to open our mouths. Months later I sat at my computer in my parents' house and I typed her name in the search box. Johannas popped up but none were her. I used the email she had given me but never received a response. When I dialed her number I reached a recording that stated that the party was no longer available. I needed to know she was okay. I needed to know she was alive, that she made it, that we could make it. But I lost her.

Leo marched the halls with psychiatrically approved iPod buds in his ears. Sometimes he played imaginary instruments, like a drunk man in a bar strumming his invisible strings to his favorite Bon Jovi song. He always wore a brown tweed jacket with a bit of paint on it and basketball shorts, sometimes inside out. He liked to paint his face with blue and green paint. His way in was interesting—he lay down in a busy intersection in California and refused to move.

I was sitting at one of the wooden tables in front of the nurses' station one afternoon when I heard it. I could hear Leo screaming from the end of the hall.

"Who was in my room! Who the fuck went in my room?!"

The staff jumped up from behind their station and rushed to him, feet racing on blue carpet.

"You fucking pigs! You have no right. It's mine. You are fucking pigs. I hate you! I hate this fucking place!"

There was sound from Michael, one of the nurses, but I couldn't make out his words.

"No. Please," Leo begged. "I'm sorry. Please don't."

They did it anyway, pierced his skin with a thin piece of metal injecting silence. Moments later he came to the main room in tears, passed the nurse a number written on a small piece of paper and asked her to dial his father.

The call did not go through.

Without a word I moved to him and placed my hand on his back. He looked up at me as tears slid down his face, turning green as they ran over the paint on his cheeks.

"Will you be okay?" I asked. He nodded.

"You're beautiful, you know?" he said. "Don't let anyone tell you any different. Don't ever try to kill yourself again. Promise me…Promise me."

I smiled. What I had done just days prior was beyond my comprehension. How could I say "I won't" when the answer might one day become "I will"?

"Thank you for checking on me," he said.

How long had it been since he had been shown love? Was he pushed away as he changed from whoever he had once been to who he had become?

"I need to go to my room," he said. His voice poured out of his mouth like thick syrup from a glass jar as the medicine kicked in. He would soon be in a deep sleep, one of my fellow night dwellers finally in the dark.

Marcus was mean. Fighting with the nurses was how he spent his time and every day, multiple times a day, they threatened to revoke his privilege to use the smokers' room. It seemed to keep him in check but didn't stop him from getting too loud or riled up. Sometimes they threatened him with medication—poisons that erase you. Silenced. There were few people he chose to talk to, but I was one of them. He did not smile, he didn't laugh, he was only an angry storm on the sea. He had been placed on the ward after he was arrested. He wouldn't tell me why. He ate with me from time to time; we killed minutes.

"Do you smoke?" he asked as we sat at a table.

I was tearing the paper off a blue crayon. Lagoon. I had already torn it off forest and cayenne.

"Yeah," I said. "Not much, but I had been having a cigarette or two after work with my roommate. I bought a pack of American Spirits on my way out here from Oklahoma."

"That's what I smoke. If you want, I can roll you one." He was looking at his hands, picking at a scab on his left thumb.

"Sure," I said and dropped the crayon back into the basket.

He walked to the nurses' station and asked for his rolling papers and tobacco and lighter. I followed him into the room with glass walls, a terrarium for smokers. I watched his long fingers as they expertly rolled up a cigarette and handed it to me. He rolled one for himself and then lit his paper, then mine. I took a drag and tried to smile. He nodded but his lips didn't move.

The thing was, I never believed Marcus was a bad or particularly violent guy. I think he was so tired of being misunderstood that the frustration manifested into a rage against those who didn't understand, those who couldn't. Like the rest of us he had an illness no one could see. The madness lived inside each of our brains, tucked away in gray matter.

The youngest of us, Tiffany, was barely old enough to be considered an adult. Her golden hair fell past her shoulders and shined when she sat next to the window; sunlight danced off her head. Her eyes were filled with a sadness, a darkness, as though she were lying on the bottom of the ocean. She left three days after I arrived. Her mother, a small woman with the same hair, carried Tiffany's suitcase out the double doors. From time to time I wondered if she was alive, if she could swim hard enough. Was there hope? Is there a light for such darkness?

My family had brought in my toiletries—shampoo, face wash, toothpaste. They brought them before I woke, in the days before I became conscious of my surroundings, when I was so sedated it was as though I slept while walking, while I met ghosts in my dreams. Each morning and evening I would stand by the desk waiting for a nurse to notice me, then request what I needed. I would be handed my shampoo in a tiny paper cup, name scrawled across the packaging in black marker. It was dangerous to trust me with the whole bottle. I may off myself with it. Death by Herbal Essence. It made us feel small and the staff didn't care. They were hardened by years behind that desk; worn down by the tide that washed up the mentally ill.

My throat was still sore from being intubated in ICU so my family brought popsicles to the psych ward to soothe the irritation. A nurse wrote my name on the box and stored them in a freezer inaccessible to patients, but promised me all I needed to do if I wanted one was ask. Each night I waited at the desk as the nurses typed furiously on keyboards, oblivious to me standing there, arms folded on the counter. I cleared my throat, they looked annoyed. How could I bother them? How dare I have needs? I had to plead, always. That is life in a psych ward: begging for popsicles at three in the morning from someone who hates you for being alive.

Because I had intentionally tried to kill myself, I was involuntarily admitted into the hospital. How long I would stay there was up to the doctors. When I would no longer be a threat to myself or anyone else I could go home. I could not check myself out, nor could my family. I spent days in the psych ward that became my new world. The psychiatrist assigned to my case and medication management shared my first name. What a cruel joke. If we shared a name, did we both share the key to my freedom? There were numerous meetings in my mind like a fog that forms above a warmer sea.

"How are you feeling?" Elena asked me, her voice thick with a European accent.

"I'm all right," I said. "Still confused,"

"Well, you're very depressed," she said, without looking up.

"But I wasn't depressed last week. I was fine. I was happy," I said. "But now, now I feel horrible."

"I have you on some antidepressants, they should help. How are you sleeping?"

"I'm not. The sleep medicine isn't working. I get about two hours of sleep a night and I am exhausted."

"Well, I'll increase the dosage. I'll see you tomorrow."

Those meetings were not therapy sessions but merely an exchange of information—brisk and without emotion. The word bipolar was never mentioned. The thought of a manic episode was never brought up. At the time my sudden suicide attempt was simply without explanation.

I worked with a patient advocate who spoke to me about my rights and my impending hearing. I met with a caseworker, Kerry, who shared information with not only me but also my family. I remember my father's anger. He displayed his confusion in loud words during a family meeting with Kerry.

"I don't understand. Why did she do this?" he asked Kerry. Then he turned to me, "Why did you do this?" His words were hard and hot and full of pain.

I looked away, focused on a cloud floating in a blue sky outside the window. I had no answer. I hurt as much as he did but was too tired emotionally and physically to imagine an answer. Sadness had taken up residence in my heart.

Finally, the day arrived when a decision would be made. Would I stay there in that sanctuary for the crazy or be released into the world under the magnified scrutiny of all who knew me? Which was better? I had no idea how the "normal" people would treat me, how I would explain the unexplainable. But I did want out. I wanted the comfort of my family. I wanted to make my own decisions. I wanted a damn cup of regular coffee.

I walked to my hearing with shoulders so weighted I could barely carry them down the hall. I sat in a small, windowless room with the four of them—my psychiatrist, my patient advocate, my caseworker, and a judge. I wore my best—a purple dress my family had packed and brought for me. My spine was a rod, my ankles a cross. The advocate explained the plan we had created. I would move in with my parents and see both a therapist and a psychiatrist. My family had already made arrangements for both, called back to Oklahoma with their pleas. I would not hurt myself. I would not hurt myself. The judge asked me a few questions, which are lost now. Options were discussed and I sat holding my breath, studying the brooch on the judge's jacket. Waiting. I was dismissed. I could go. What was left of my heart leapt.

My smile told my friends, my crazy friends, that I had made it through and would be leaving our small world to face one much bigger outside. They congratulated me. I thought I saw a twinge of regret in their eyes.

When my family came, they searched my face.

"I can go," I told them. "I can leave today."

My dad wrapped his arms around me and hugged me tightly. My mom rubbed my back as tears came to her eyes.

I packed my things—sweatpants, hospital socks, sweatshirts, photographs. I was granted my toiletries, this time bottles and tubes, not Dixie cups.

I said my goodbyes, knowing I would never see those faces again. We would all deal with our illnesses on our own. Some of us would find help. Others would self-medicate with alcohol and drugs in an effort to escape our minds. Some of us would get "better" only to stop taking our medicine and fall back down. Many would be hospitalized again. A few would only escape the madness by falling for the seduction of death. We could not see our future, we did not know what lay beneath the deep water, we only knew, as best we could remember, where we had been.

I had papers to sign and instructions to follow. I still belonged to them until I walked out the doors. We gathered my things, my flowers, with best wishes and I walked unsteadily to the door. The hall was strange. The elevator foreign. I was swimming to the shore, one arm, then the other. The silver doors part-ed and I walked into a lobby. Glass doors stood before me. We walked out and the breeze hit my face and nose, filling my lungs. A small red flower grew on a bush. I touched it. Perhaps because I needed to know it was real, or maybe just because it was alive and beautiful.

CHAPTER 2

Blog post

Sometimes, well all the time, I wonder how much I should share on my blog. This is my place to share, to figure things out while I type and perhaps more than anything to allow others to know that they are not the only ones out there who feel a certain way or that they deal with life alone. To be honest do you have to give everything up, throw up your soul? I believe authenticity starts by no longer pretending to be anyone other than yourself, which includes hiding who you are or putting a pretty smile on your pretty face and telling the world, "Everything is all right!"

But sometimes our insides are not as pretty as that smile. Often they are twisted and bruised and, perhaps, bleeding. And what would happen if we were exposed and the world could see us, see that "horrible" inside? My guess is that if we all were stripped down, vulnerable, we would find that most of us don't look all that different from anyone else.

What is our desire to shine one hundred percent of the time? Even the stars fade. We cannot falter. We must be perfect.

Before the Crazy Came

Let me start at the beginning, because in order to under-stand who I am, you must first understand who I was. There is no here without there. Bipolar disorder has changed me. I am not the person I set out to be. This wasn't part of the plan. But I couldn't know that back then. I couldn't see the madness. I didn't know it was there, hiding, waiting.

I was born a military brat in Japan in 1981. I don't remember the country; we left before I was two, but it made for an interesting fact. Guess where I was born? Go ahead, guess. We moved a lot when I was young, from country to country, state to state. It was easy for me. Exciting. Although I was always sad to leave my friends, I was at ease making new ones. There were slumber parties and scavenger hunts, forts and secret clubs. As a small child there was no premonition of the struggles that lie ahead; it wouldn't be until junior high that I experienced depressive symptoms. Back then it was only sunshine or hot chocolate with marshmallows, parents to hold my hand and a grandma who loved me.

School was always easy. As soon as I was able I devoured words. I read all the time. I created a library at home and forced my cousins to check out books. I would sit in the back of the car reading billboards out loud as we passed by. My hunger was insatiable. At six years old I wrote a letter to my teacher telling her I was sometimes bored in class and asked her to give me more work. I had an extra spelling list in addition to the one required by the rest of my class. I didn't want to waste time. I wanted to learn. In the second grade my teacher quickly recognized my intellect and met with my parents to discuss moving me up to the third grade early. I sat through endless tests, which were followed by a slow integration with the older students. I took some subjects with the third graders and spent some of the school day with my peers. Halfway through the school year I was moved up completely, leaving my friends behind. The day I skipped up to the third grade there was a knock on my front door. My dad answered it. He came into the living room and told me that there was someone there for me. When I got to the door I found my neighbor Peter standing there.

"Is it true you skipped a grade?" he asked.

"Yes," I said. "Today."

"Okay, cool," he said, and walked away.

And that's how it was. The third graders were interested in me and the move, and they accepted me. Skipping a year of school didn't slow me down. I was placed in classes for the gifted and met with a teacher with white hair that changed color. Sometimes it was a shade of blue, other times it was slightly pink. My mom told me it was a rinse with which she washed her hair. I thought it was fascinating.

I enjoyed performing. I joined a British musical theater group while living in England. I played little Puss in Boots one year and a villager in the Wizard of Oz the next. I liked being on stage, having all eyes on me. I always auditioned for the school talent show, creating dance routines with my friends. I craved attention. Performing brought me accolades. I believe attention fueled my brain. The more I excelled in school, the more attention I received. It motivated me to work hard. If I made good grades my parents would take me out for a special dinner without my brother and sister. I cherished those evenings. I remember them still, sitting in dark restaurants, ordering like an adult.

I grew up the middle of three children. My brother is twenty months older and we got along well. He was my first playmate and a constant as we moved around. He took on the role of big brother proudly, and watched out for me.

My sister is three and a half years younger, and I adored her. I remember the day she was born. I can still feel the hand of our neighbor as she led me to her house so my parents could head to the hospital. I remember holding my baby sister in my arms for the first time. With that first glance, I fell in love. We were always close. As children we made up plays and performed them for our parents. We played Barbies. We played house. We sat side by side and watched cartoons. On Christmas Eve we would snuggle in the same bed listening for Santa and his reindeer until our dad would threaten that Santa wouldn't come unless we went to sleep. As we grew up we only grew closer. She looked up to me.

She wanted to be like me. I didn't want to disappoint her.

In junior high I joined the school drill team. I practiced hard, shaking my pom-poms and kicking high into the air. The girls on the team became my best friends. I loved performing our routines on the football field for a cheering crowd and competing against other drill teams in the area. By the time I reached high school the school's drill team had dissolved. I joined a community dance team and though I missed the football game halftimes, I still loved the competitions we took part in.

It was in junior high that I experienced my first depressive symptoms. They came and they went. I didn't speak to anyone about them. I hid them deep down where no one could see them. I didn't know they were a prelude of things to come. I believed if I could just be everything people wanted, if I could just be perfect, the darkness would leave me alone.

In high school, I set my sights on cheerleading. I tried out for the freshman squad and was crushed when I didn't make it. It was the first time I had really failed at something. When the call came from the coach that I didn't make it on the squad I couldn't hear her tell me to try out again; all I could hear was "you're not good enough."

My best friend made the squad and I spent my freshman year watching her sashay through the hallways in her short, pleated skirt. I wanted to be one of them, the popular girls, so badly. As the end of freshman year approached I again tried out to be a cheerleader for my sophomore year. This time I made it. I loved cheering for the soccer reserve team. I loved wearing my uniform to school on game days. I loved making favors for the players. I loved the attention.

I was a member of a lot of clubs in high school; so many I can't remember them all. Drama, choir, cheerleading, dance team. I wanted to be everything. I wanted to be perfect. And all the while I participated in extracurricular activities, I studied hard. I was in advanced classes and maintained an A-B average.

In my junior year I joined NJROTC (Navy Junior Reserve Officer Training Corp). It was the inaugural year for the program at the school and my friends and I decided it might be fun. Once a week we were required to wear our uniforms to school. The first day I was so embarrassed. The uniform was uncool, and I wanted to be anything but uncool. But I wore it and the only teasing I received was good-natured. One day a week I was wearing a cheerleading uniform, one day a week I was wearing a military uniform. I became the public affairs officer, a leader in the program. I joined the drill team and air rifle team. I excelled in the environment and my senior year I was chosen to be the commanding officer in charge of ninety-some other students. The class would stand at attention when I walked into the room. They listened as I performed uniform inspections. I attended leadership academy for two weeks in the summer at Great Lakes in Chicago and was recognized as one of the top cadets. When it came time to decide what I wanted to do in the future I decided I wanted to be a military jet pilot. When I found out during a physical that my eyesight would prevent me from pursuing that career, I felt lost. At the end of my senior year I was offered a college scholarship from the Navy and one from the Air Force. I turned both down.

With my jet pilot dreams dashed, I was left staring into the abyss of my future. I thought about what I enjoyed and what I was good at. I landed on fashion magazines. Since before I was a teenager I had subscribed to magazines—YM, Seventeen, Jane. I loved reading them and would stare at the fashion spreads in wonder. I had always had a love of clothes. Often my friends would invite me to go shopping with them and listen to my advice on what to wear. And I was good at writing. I had always been in advanced English classes and when I read a short story to a class the teacher asked me if I had considered becoming an author. I began to think more seriously about writing. I wrote letters to several women's magazines asking for advice on what to study in college—fashion, journalism, English? I received responses and they all told me to study what I wanted, but to get as much writing experience as I could.

At the time of graduation, I was living in Ohio. During the

fall of my senior year, my dad had been transferred to Oklahoma. My parents decided that my mom would stay behind in Ohio so that she would be around for my brother during his first year out of the house, so that I could finish high school, and so that my sister could finish junior high at our current schools. I applied to colleges in Ohio, Colorado, and Oklahoma. I applied to journalism programs at all except for Oklahoma State University. There I applied for the apparel design and production program. I was accepted to all and received scholarship offers from each school. In the end I chose Oklahoma State University. With the scholarships they offered it was the most affordable and I was so intrigued with the idea of studying fashion that I couldn't resist.

When I started my freshman year I didn't know anyone at the school. In fact, I only knew three people in the whole state—my mother, my father, and my sister—and they lived an hour and a half away. I lived in a dorm and didn't have a car so I only saw my family when they came to visit. It was a lonely time in the beginning. I bonded with my suitemates in the dorm and slowly got to know the other girls in the fashion program. I got a work-study job at the college recreation center and supervised the weight room. It wasn't a bad job, watching college hot bodies pump iron. I joined my college's student council as the publicity chair and wrote monthly newsletters. I wrote for the university newspaper. Meanwhile I learned to sew in class and spent a lot of time in the sewing lab. Over the course of my college career much time would be spent in the lab, sewing late into the night.

At the end of my sophomore year I applied for an internship at W magazine, a high-fashion magazine based in New York City. I decided to be creative in my application for the internship and turned my submission into a mini-magazine. My cover letter was the letter from the editor, my resume was a profile piece, articles I'd written for school became features, and my references were letters to the editor. I am not sure if it was my submission or my persistent badgering of the internship contact that got me the job, but the summer after my sophomore year I was living in Times Square.

I was nineteen years old when I went to New York City. I had never been there before, except for when we flew into JFK when we returned from England when I was twelve. I remember coming up from Penn Station onto the street. People rushed around. Cars honked their horns. Everything was different, so different from Oklahoma and everywhere I had ever been. One of my best friends had landed a wardrobe internship with MTV that summer and we ended up living across the hall from each other in a building for students in Times Square. My room was crowded, with four loft beds with desks below them, a bathroom, a sink and microwave, a table, a television, and four young women. But I didn't spend much time there. I was always at work or out exploring the city with my best friend. The first week of my job was pure intimidation. Everyone looked like they had walked out of a fashion magazine in their sleek, black clothes and shiny, straight hair while I showed up to work in lavender skirts and kitten heels, curly hair bouncing.

My job as a wardrobe intern was to work in the closet, a tiny room where all the clothing and accessories for photo shoots were received, organized, stored, and returned. That tiny room stored hundreds of thousands of dollars' worth of clothing. There were a few highlights of my summer at W. First, I was allowed to assist editors for two fashion photo shoots. One was for high-profile men in the media, another for a famous actress. Near the end of the summer I was given a reporting job for Women's Wear Daily, the fashion industry's daily newspaper. I was told to interview women on the street about bathing suits for a special publication. I was excited when the article came out and my name was glowing on the page. That summer was pivotal. I fell in love with New York City, with its energy and character. I loved the food and the museums and the parks and the shops. When I went home, I couldn't wait to go back.

My junior year went by quickly—one day the leaves were falling, the next there were purple buds on the trees. It was during this winter in 2000 that I experienced an unparalleled depression and was introduced to antidepressants. I was required to find a design internship the summer before my senior year, and landed a job at Liz Claiborne in New York City. I was delighted that this internship paid ten dollars an hour, unlike the unpaid one the summer before. I found an apartment in Brooklyn with a good friend from high school who was in college in Ohio at the time. She was completing an internship at Capitol Records and it was her first summer in New York City. The apartment turned out to be in a rough neighborhood and the lack of air conditioning in ninety-degree weather had me melting. The bathroom was impossibly small and I could wash my face in the sink while sitting on the toilet. But we were in New York City, so we stayed out of the apartment. Our shade from the heat came in the form of hours at the Guggenheim or American Museum of Natural History. Our kitchen became happy hours that offered half-price appetizers. I excelled in my internship and designed a jacket that was produced. Although I was good at flat-sketching garments, computer-aided design, and creating inspiration boards, I felt that I was out of touch with people. So much time was spent doing my work at a computer that there was little communication. I missed the magazine industry. At the end of the summer, I had decided. I would move to New York after graduation and look for a job at a magazine.

If my junior year moved fast, my senior year flew by faster. School kept me busy and I had been elected president of my college's student council. In addition, I was still working as a publications assistant for my college for twenty hours a week in between classes. I had held the job since my sophomore year and loved it and my boss. I juggled all of it at the end of the year as I applied for jobs in New York City. That summer, after graduation, I moved to the big city.

Finding a job in fashion wasn't easy, so I took a job as a hostess at a new Argentinean restaurant in midtown. I found a townhouse to rent with the same girl I had lived with the summer before. We found a third roommate and moved in. In the fall I got a lead on a temporary position with a prestigious fashion public relations firm. I was hired to help out during New York Fashion Week. I was enthralled with the beauty and glamour of the scene. I would work with the company for five seasons, fall and spring, and assisted at great lengths on designer fashion shows.

After that first fall Fashion Week I got a freelance job at an event production company. Because of the excitement of the fashion shows, my interest in event planning and production grew. I helped out with a few projects, one at a fine jewelry store on Madison Avenue, another at an event in Colorado. The projects were glamorous, but I missed the fashion world. After a brief stint at as a coat check girl—a grueling and thankless job—I went to a temp agency looking for work. A week later I was sitting in the Victoria's Secret Catalogue offices. I worked in the sweater department. The hours were demanding, and I made a lot of cash in overtime. But I didn't want to be a designer, and working as a design assistant was unfulfilling. I worked there as a temp for six months. When my lease was up, I moved back to Oklahoma.

Back home with my parents I got a couple of part-time jobs working retail at the mall. I was bored and wanted to go back to New York City, but would not move back permanently without a job there. I went back that fall temporarily for Fashion Week and during an event bumped into a girl I had interned with at W. She introduced me to an editor at Cosmopolitan and I landed an interview for a position as an accessories assistant. I didn't get the job, but without my knowledge she passed my resume on to a friend who was hiring an assistant for a new start-up women's magazine.

Back in Oklahoma I received a call from the fashion editor, who told me about the position and that she was also from Oklahoma. I told her that if she gave me the job I could be there in a week. I got the job.

A week later I was sleeping on my sister's ex-boyfriend's couch in the East Village. The next day I went out and found a room to rent on the Upper West Side. I fell in love with my job. I called fashion houses and PR firms for clothing samples. I organized the closet. I wrote copy. I brainstormed ideas. I attended fashion events representing the magazine. We worked on the start-up for four months before it was canceled. I was so disappointed.

I went back to Oklahoma for a few months. The managing editor from the start-up emailed me to let me know he was sub-leasing his place for half a year. A studio on the Upper West Side for six hundred dollars a month was too good to pass up. I moved back and got a job at Starbucks, then landed a job at Budget Living magazine as a fashion assistant. I was in my element. But when it came time for the managing editor to return to his apartment I decided it was time to leave New York City for good. It was a hard life there, a constant struggle to stay afloat. I decided I would, I could, only live there if I was making a lot more money than my current positions could pay, so I set my sights on Austin, Texas, another city I had never been to. I had read good things and decided a change of pace would be in order.

I got a job as an assistant editor at a lifestyle magazine in Austin a couple months later. I got a big apartment, nearly three times as big as the studio I had been living in during my last stay in New York City. It took some time to slow down. I was so used to the frenetic pace of the big city. I settled into Texas life and grew in my job. I began to write features for the magazine and remembered why it was that I loved to write. Styling fashion photo shoots was still a favorite part of the job, and at every opportunity I wrote a fashion story. I made a name for myself attending Austin events—store openings, fashion shows, balls, art exhibits. I was always out, moving and shaking.

Then a fashion styling opportunity fell in my lap. A makeup artist I worked with recommended me to MTV to style the press photos for the cast of The Real World: Austin. It was my first big styling job on my own, and one that gave me national press. My relationships with local store owners allowed me to borrow the needed clothing and accessories. I met with the cast then styled them in five outfits each the day of the shoot. It was incredible that I was being paid five hundred dollars a day for something I loved to do.

One day my boss at the magazine came to me with a new task. He had made a deal with a local radio station to create a weekly fashion segment, "The Friday Fashion Fix with Elaina Martin." I would come up with weekly fashion trend advice and do a giveaway to a local shop. Having never been on the radio before, the first time live was nerve-wracking. Luckily, the segment was a success and I would keep the position for the next two years, even after I left the magazine.

A little over a year after I started at the Austin magazine, my boss called me into a meeting. He had visited my Myspace page and read my blog. He was concerned that I was writing about my personal life and asked me to be careful. I was annoyed that he was spying on me and took his warning under consideration. The following week I wrote a post about how my blog was being read by everyone, including my boss. The next morning, I came into work to find my boss, who was usually not in the office, there waiting for me. He called me into the conference room and told me he had read my blog and that he felt it made him look bad. I was irate at his ego. Then, he fired me. I walked the mile home to my apartment in a state of shock. I couldn't believe that a benign blog had got me fired. I never wrote anything remotely risqué or scandalous. A few months later I turned my blog and subsequent firing into a story for a national women's magazine and was paid over a thousand dollars for it.

I lived off of unemployment for a couple of months. I had to get rid of my nice apartment and move into a tiny studio, one that I could afford. Soon after the move I got a job at another lifestyle magazine based in Austin. This one was a luxury publication for the entire state of Texas. I was the executive editor there, a promotion from my last position. It was hard work. Late hours and some weekends. But I was able to write and that made it worth it. The highlight of the job was travel writing. I flew to Sweden, the Bahamas, Mexico, Belize, the British Virgin Island, and Turks & Caicos, and stayed at fabulous resorts to write a story about each. It was amazing.

I was there for a little over a year before the stress of the position proved too much. At Christmas time I resigned on good terms with the publisher. I took a job at a local elite gym where

Austin's celebrities worked out. It was a good move, though I was making far less money. I enjoyed greeting gym members, being a good part of their day. I lost the fifteen pounds I had gained working at the magazine. For a moment, I was happy.

And there was where the madness came. It whispered at first: the darkness that had hovered over my head from time to time, the cuts, the occasional hopelessness. It came and it went. I hadn't learned about mania yet, though looking back there were hints of it. I didn't know yet how bad it would get, what it would rob of me, that I would become someone else. It would all become a memory of better days, days when I was strong. I had been a superstar, exceeding expectations, running fast and hard. It would all change. This is my story...

CHAPTER 3

In 1993, at age 12, I wrote this poem:

Even though I am loved

I feel so all alone

But I try not to complain

I try not to moan.

I know they all care for me

In their own dear way

I still feel all alone

Disliked I dare say.

They lecture because I don't smile

And when I do they yell

They ask me how I feel

But yet I do not tell.

I don't tell how I'm all alone

About this hollowness inside

I try to act as if I'm strong

My weak side I do hide.

My emotions do not lead me

Instead I use my brain

I act as if I am just a rock

As if I do not feel pain.

I don't know how long I'll last

Or when my rock will crumble

I don't know when my emotions will lead me

Or when all my words will fumble.

I will keep this emptiness to myself

For now I will be strong

I will smile my smile

I just don't know for how long.

Coming Up with a Plan

I don't remember the first time I thought about dying. That would be like trying to remember your first breath or the last time you blinked. I now know that there was always a silent dwelling of dark thoughts. When my sister and I were little our imaginations would take hold of our small bodies. We didn't need toys, only each other to play. Her golden ringlets would bounce as we imitated adults and storybook characters.

"Pretend I died," I said, lying on the rust-colored carpet with one eye open, hands over my chest trying as hard as I could not to breathe, and to appear as dead as an eight-year-old is able.

"Elaina, I don't want to," my sister said.

"Come on, just pretend to cry."

"No," she said. "It makes me sad."

"I'm not really dead, silly. It's just pretend."

"Let's play house instead."

"Okay."

When my brother, sister and I weren't playing I had too much time to think. In the back of our minivan my ten-year-old self would look out the window and wonder if maybe I was on my death bed, maybe my life was nothing but a series of memories. I was old, dying. My hair was silver and sparse and my skin thin, nearly transparent. Propped up on pillows, covered in thick blankets to keep my bones warm, I was perhaps closing my eyes. Nothing left to offer the world; nothing left to live, my life reduced to thoughts of days gone by, perhaps of a young girl sitting in the back of a minivan with her family. My life had been determined, the course set and in the end I was nothing more than a weak old woman lying on a pile of what had been.

Often I would sit wondering how long I would live, how many years God would grant me. Five, twenty, sixty? There was always an expiration date stamped on my life; I just couldn't read the numbers.

No one knew that I fixated on death at eleven years old, that I wanted it as much as I had ever wanted anything. I was everything that was asked of me—straight As, student council. I was trying so hard to be so damn perfect. I didn't wear black clothing or dye my hair to match it. I didn't hang out with a certain "bad" crowd. I wasn't smoking cigarettes or pot, and I wasn't drinking. To the naked eye everything was fine; to the naked eye it was perfect.

One day I snapped, when something inside me said, "Enough of Ms. Perfect!" I was sitting in Mr. Delk's social studies class trying to pay attention as he rambled on about the Civil War. David sat on my desk.

"Get off my desk," I whispered.

He turned back and looked at me and smiled. He didn't move.

Time crawled by and my temper rose. Slowly and with purpose I pulled my protractor from math class out of my bag. I held the shiny metal weapon in my hand and stabbed him in the back.

"Ow! What the heck!" David yelled as he jumped off my desk and stood next to his seat rubbing the place I had pierced him.

Class stopped.

"What's going on?" Mr. Delk asked.

"Someone stabbed me in the back!" David said.

Immediately Mr. Delk fixed his eyes on a known troublemaker named Derrick.

I took a deep breath. "It was me," I said. I waited for my punishment, to be sent to the principal's office, to be relegated to detention. I couldn't think of anything worse than a phone call to my parents. But after a long pause a smile crept over my teacher's face.

"Well," Mr. Delk said. "Let that be a lesson to you all; don't mess with Elaina."

And no one messed with me. No one bothered to see what was below the surface, below the braces and lipgloss. No one could see down to my beating heart.

I wasn't part of the elite crowd but I was popular enough. I had friends to talk to on the phone in my pink bedroom, enough friends to invite to my birthday party. We'd spend hours at the mall. There were parties and sleepovers. I had a crush on Anthony, my older brother's friend. He lived down the street and rode my bus. I liked the way his smile made his green eyes crinkle up and the way he parted his mousy brown hair. He was already taller than most of the boys in the eighth grade and that made me like him more. When I broke the growth plate in my elbow he carried my books for me between classes and I relished every time the bell would ring.

But they weren't enough. The friends. The crush. The good grades. They weren't enough. There was in me a hole, a dark abyss growing larger every day, threatening to suck me in. How long could I fool everyone? How long could I pretend that anything mattered, anything at all? The weight of my life was becoming unbearable. I was trying so hard to be perfect, but I didn't know that no one expected me to be. I didn't know then that it was okay to fail.

I brought home a report card with its row of As and was taken out to dinner. Just me. My brother and sister were left at home. I had my parents' undivided attention. I loved those dinners spent drinking Shirley Temples in dimly lit restaurants. Speaking without interruption. Chewing my food quickly just so I could open my mouth and let all my words march out. In the seventh grade I was still in love with those nights and worked hard just so I could have another one of them, so I could have a few hours of my parents' time. Our house was noisy and family dinners were filled with animated conversation. I loved my siblings but I craved attention and I asked for it passively through all that I did. Look what I've done. Isn't it impressive? Aren't you proud of me? Don't I make you smile? I was the classic middle child, always mediating, making sure things went smoothly, ironically invisible. I wanted to be seen yet wanted to disappear. Forever.

My parents came to my Saturday dance competitions. I donned a sparkly leotard and dancer's tights. I prepped in a classroom, the taste of hairspray in the air. On the gym floor I came alive. I shook my pom-poms, shook my hips. I kicked my heels higher than my head to the cheers of the crowd. Kick it, girls! The other dance team members were my best friends. They told me their secrets, but I was afraid to let anyone see the darkness inside me. I was afraid I would push them away. The hole grew larger.

It was during my seventh grade year that I came up with my first suicide plan. At eleven there weren't a lot of options. I had no access to guns or knives beyond the kitchen. There were no pills within reach save the ibuprofen in the bathroom closet. I knew that those white pills wouldn't do the job. I needed something sure, something that could permanently take me away from my life.

My school sat at the bottom of a hill on National Road. It was a major street and big trucks and cars flew by at speeds of 50 or more miles per hour. There were trees on the side of the road just before the school; in front of the building were bushes. Here is where I planned to hide and wait for a truck to come. When it approached the bottom of the hill I would run from the bushes into the road. It would be fast. It would be over.

The problem was opportunity. I didn't know how I could get outside to the road without being caught, because as much as I wanted to end my life I did not want to get in trouble. And then one day I had my moment. I was standing in the hall after using the pass to go to the bathroom. The halls were empty. There were no teachers, no students. Only me and my pounding heart. I walked past the trophy case. There was a poster asking me to vote for a friend for student council.

I got as far as the door.

The one flaw I saw in my plan, the flaw I had seen all along, lay with the driver. I kept seeing his face as he hit me. He would, for the rest of his life, be a man who had killed a child. His guilt would be unbearable. I couldn't live or die with that. I walked back to my class and knew that I would never realize my fantasy.

In time my mood lifted. Months later the gaping hole began to close. I could step over it. Occasionally I would fall into it and when I did I thought of the road. I don't know if it would have worked. I just needed to believe that I had an out. After eighth grade I moved across the tennis courts to the high school. With me moved the plan. I never got further than that moment by the doors when I hesitated. As I grew up the ways to kill myself changed—pills and knives and guns. But like a first love I will never forget the longing I felt then, the ease with which I decided to say goodbye to my life.

CHAPTER 4

Blog post

Have you ever felt beautiful? Alone. No one whispering in your ear, no gazing into your eyes. Simply being. A walk in the grass, a stare to the stars. I feel that way today and it is a rarity. I have no makeup, no fancy dress, just the sun on my shoulders and kissing my face. The breeze is light, barely rolling over my skin. Whether you are 90 pounds or 300 you can feel it. Sometimes it is brief, just a moment of confidence in who you are, other times it holds your head high and places a smile on your lips. It isn't about going out to find a man or impress anyone else. It isn't about pride or vanity. It is the beauty of love for oneself. A split second or more when you feel things are right and you are exactly who you should be.

Bent Over Porcelain

I bent over the porcelain bowl at my best friend's grandparents' house in North Dakota. My right index finger passed teeth straightened by years of braces and a soft pink tongue. I felt my stomach seize. My eyes watered and I did it again, this time touching my tonsil. With a retch up came the mashed potatoes and chicken I had only minutes earlier consumed, the meal my best friend's grandmother had made for me. I pulled some toilet paper off the roll and dabbed at my eyes where the tears had smeared the black eyeliner and blacker mascara. I tossed the toilet paper in the toilet and pushed down on the shiny silver handle. I watched my dinner disappear and ran a hand over my stomach. I would not get fat. I would not get fat.

It started when I was sixteen. I had gained a little weight while on vacation with my best friend's family. At sixteen I had very little control over what I ate and when, especially while on vacation. If I tried to avoid a meal altogether I drew attention, and I didn't want that kind of attention. I wanted to be perfect without needs or noise.

I had already tried restrictions. No fat. No French fries. Use caffeine as a major food group. I would pore over the labels of the food in our cupboards at home before I placed the contents in my mouth. But in the end, I had to eat. The hunger in my stomach would not allow me to starve. Anorexia would not work for me.

I threw up a couple more times on the trip. Once more in that baby blue bathroom and once at Jones Family Restaurant with its wallpaper of burgundy baskets on a cream background. It was easy, matter-of-fact. Eat, then throw up. Even if I didn't have the will to refuse to eat, I could still keep the food out of my stomach.

A couple of months later my boyfriend met me for lunch at school. It was my senior year and though he had graduated four months earlier, he was a former JROTC cadet so my JROTC teacher allowed us to meet in his room during lunch. He brought me a kid's meal from McDonalds. I squeezed a packet of ketchup onto my hamburger and swirled it around with my finger. Then I put my finger in my mouth and sucked the sweet, tangy condiment off. One by one I ate my fries, saving the softest ones for the end of my meal. They were my favorite. When I was done eating I waited, watching the clock, thinking of the food in my stomach. I worried that it was making me fat and excused myself to the bathroom. I walked into the dimly lit bathroom and looked at the doors of the stalls to see if any of them were closed. I walked into the first stall and squatted down to look at the floor, to look for feet. I was alone. Then I bent over, put my finger into my mouth, moved it towards my throat and threw up.

It became easy. Where once it had taken several attempts fishing my finger in the back of my throat to bring my food up, eventually all I had to do was bend over the toilet and will the food up.

"You've lost a lot of weight," Tony said as we stood in the empty JROTC room. Already I had to get a smaller size uniform because of the weight I had dropped.

"Thanks," I was ecstatic. People were beginning to notice. It was reinforcement. Keep it up, Elaina. It garners compliments and smiles and approval. Throwing up is making you a better person; a better, thinner version of yourself.

I learned what foods came up easy—ice cream and pasta, and which were harder to vomit—pizza and meat. I learned that lettuce floated in the toilet bowl and was hard to flush away. I planned my meals around the ease of which I could get rid of it after eating.

The first time I saw a counselor, it was to get help with my eating disorder. I went away to college and the eating disorder came along uninvited. Before college I had vomited normal sized meals but at school I began to binge. I would eat three desserts in the cafeteria knowing—planning—to throw it up as soon as I got back to my dorm room and the bathroom I shared with my suitemate.

Eating disorders are about control, and for me that also meant controlling my weight. But by the time I got to college, with over a year of disordered eating under my belt, it was controlling me. I couldn't eat without throwing up. I was scared to death to sit still after a meal.

I sat in the waiting area of the university counseling center and fidgeted with my green Jansport backpack on my lap. I was finally doing it. I was going to get help. I had finished filling out the required forms asking me questions about depression and mood as well as about my academic coursework. Had I ever sought counseling before? Did I plan on hurting myself?

I was hurting myself—every time I ate.

There were ten chairs covered in orange upholstery in the waiting area. On the walls were inspirational posters on leadership and determination. I unzipped and zipped the small pocket of my bag over and over again until a pretty blonde girl looked at me, then my hands, then back at my eyes. Five minutes later a petite young woman with black hair called my name and I followed her back to a small room. It was dim with only a desk lamp on, and the shades on the window were closed.

"I'm Michelle," she said with a smile. "What brings you to the university counseling center?"

"Well, I've been making myself throw up and I don't want to do it anymore but I can't stop."

"How long have you been doing this?" she asked.

"It started the summer before last. I stopped for a while, but once I got here it started again."

"How often are you vomiting?"

"Up to three times a day. It depends on what I eat. I can't seem to stop myself from eating," I told her.

We spoke for twenty minutes about not only my eating but also about my stress level, how I was adjusting to college, and how I was feeling. When we finished talking I scheduled an appointment for two weeks later.

When I saw Michelle again we did an exercise. I was given a sheet of paper with five silhouettes of a woman's body on it. Each one more plump than the previous one. I was told to pick out the body that most looked like mine. I stared at the sheet for a minute and chose the second to last image. Because I was, after all, fat. Michelle took the sheet from me and told me that I had body dysmorphia, meaning that I didn't see my body as it actually was. She pointed to the second body on the page and told me that it was an accurate depiction of me, not the body two sizes larger that I had selected. She told me that although my symptoms were a lot like a bulimic's I had an "eating disorder otherwise unclassified" because my vomiting did not always follow a binge.

"What do you think about when you are bent over the toilet?" she asked.

"I don't want to be fat," I said.

The third time I saw Michelle I lied to her. The problem was that I liked Michelle. I liked her so much that I did not want to disappoint her. So, when she asked me if I had thrown up, I told her that I hadn't. That made her smile and praise me. That was the last time I saw her. I figured I didn't need to spend time lying to someone else about my eating disorder. I was doing enough of that already.

My desire to vomit came and went. Sometimes I could resist the urge for weeks at a time and then one day my pants would feel tight and I would begin to do it again. It wasn't that I didn't try to diet, it was just that I didn't have to willpower I wanted to decline food altogether. I wanted to see bones instead of flesh. I wanted to be skinny.

During my sophomore year I lived just off-campus in a duplex with one of my suitemates from freshman year. The house was old and the backyard would flood into the kitchen when it rained hard and long. My room was a converted garage just off the kitchen and I shared it with my collie, Freedom. With my roommate often gone I was free to gorge. I sat down with a box of Raisin Bran Crunch and ate bowl after bowl. I got up from the table and walked around the tiny hall to the bathroom and threw up. Then I sat back down and ate some more.

Then in my junior year I fell in love again. Nick excelled academically and socially. He was the student council president the year before I was and often we were neck and neck for awards given by the college. He was generous, buying drinks for all my friends at Eskimo Joe's, a local hangout. He bought me gifts from Tiffany & Co. We spent a weekend with his parents at their lake house. He seemed to know the right thing to say and the right thing to do, as though someone had given him the instruction manual to life while the rest of us were searching for clues on what to do next. I fell in love with him and imagined a life that included a wedding and children and politics. As my happiness grew, my eating disorder shrank. I was careful about what I ate but no longer binged, no longer threw up. I grew thinner and became confident in my body. I enjoyed the curve of my hips and the flat plane of my stomach.

The summer before our senior year Nick went away to Europe. While there, he cheated on me. When he came back I met him at the airport in New York City where I was completing an internship that summer. I took one look at his face and guessed what had happened. We broke up.

The eating disorder didn't return right away. It hid in the shadows for a while, threatening to appear every time I put something fattening or sugary sweet in my mouth. During my senior year it played peek-a-boo with me. It would show up for a couple of days and then disappear again for weeks. By the time graduation rolled around it was under control. I had gone months without vomiting and looked forward to a future free from my eating disorder.

For a couple of years, I was free. The only time I bent over the porcelain bowl was when I was sick. It was liberating to eat and enjoy my food. I didn't have to worry about hiding in a bathroom after meals. And my weight leveled out at about twenty pounds more than my skinniest days. I had curves and though I wished I could be thinner, I accepted myself.

The next time I would deal with my eating disorder was after I found myself in an abusive relationship. That boyfriend's mother commented on the fact that I had gained weight and that was enough to send me right back into the waiting arms of the eating disorder. I started to eat less and less. I had a latte for breakfast, a salad for lunch, and a bagel for dinner. I didn't snack. If I had a dessert, I would throw it up. I lost fifteen pounds in a couple of months. At my smaller size I once again felt in control. I didn't need to make myself sick because I was thin enough.

I moved from New York to Austin and my eating disorder became a memory. I created a life I loved and in this new life, I learned to love myself—even the soft parts. I dieted and worked out but I no longer fell victim to my disorder.

For seven years I was someone who used to have an eating disorder. I could talk about it to my boyfriend. I could tell him about once upon a time without guilt but instead compassion. And then one night I sat down to a dinner of pizza and breadsticks with my boyfriend and his kids. I was trying to lose weight at the time. My sister's wedding was coming up in a matter of months and I needed to be thinner. There would be pictures of me. People would remember. So after I ate my third slice of pizza I left my family watching television and walked upstairs to the bathroom off of the bedroom I shared with my boyfriend. I looked at the painting of the sailboat above the toilet, then bent over the toilet, stuck my finger down my throat and threw up. I heaved several times trying to get it all up. I didn't want to keep any of it. I wanted it all gone.

It came so naturally, as though it had never gone away, like returning to a lover—knowing the curve of his shoulders and the slope of his nose in the dark. Opening your mouth to kiss and finding his warm tongue.

I did it for a couple of months. At night after dinner I would excuse myself to the bathroom. I would vomit and it was ugly. I told my therapist and at my regular appointment I also told my psychiatrist.

"Anything else I should know?" my psychiatrist asked.

"Well," I said, "I am throwing up...on purpose again."

"You've done this before?"

"Yes. It started when I was sixteen and happened on and off through college. But then, for the most part it went away. I didn't do it for years."

"Why do you think you started again?" he asked.

"I don't know. I've gained weight. I might be stressed. Instead of cutting I started throwing up. I really just traded one behavior for another."

"What does your counselor say about it?"

"We are trying to figure it out. So I can stop. I don't want to do it anymore but I can't stop," I said.

"Well, think about it this way. You were able to be in recovery for years. If you did it before, you can do it again."

He was right. This time my flirtation with my eating disorder lasted a few months. After my sister's wedding, I returned home from San Diego and slowly began to forget about throwing up my meals. I was careful not to binge. I knew that it has a lot to do with stress and my inability to handle it as much as it had to do with my weight. I gained even more weight when I stopped throwing up, but I knew that I was better off bigger than causing damage to my body. Bulimia can cause damage to your esophagus and your teeth; the acid that should be in your stomach is brought up where it doesn't belong.

According to a study by the University of Cincinnati College of Medicine published in July 2010 in the Journal of Affective Disorders, more than fourteen percent of patients with bipolar disorder also suffer from an eating disorder, and these individuals are likely to have a more severe course of illness.

I have dealt with this eating disorder on and off for over a decade. Over a fucking decade. It came before the mania and the madness. I'd like to be able to tell you it will go away completely, forever, but I know better. Even if I stop for years, it is always there, like my anxiety and my depression and my mania, just waiting for me.

CHAPTER 5

Blog post

It's there. A whisper. A hint. It is what is and what will be. He closes his eyes. He doesn't want to see it. He doesn't want to hear it. To him I am perfect.

I fall asleep before him and wake to feel him cuddled behind me. In the morning I rise to find him gone and I am alone. Alone.

There are words I shouldn't say and things I shouldn't do but they are done and I am here. There is crimson and there are smiles. There is the here and the now and we forget before and because.

There are words we don't say. Things better left alone. He doesn't know the language; he doesn't have the map. So they float between us, leaking off the page. I hug him and breathe in his scent and it is enough.

I sip my drink. I feel the water on my tongue. I think of him. How he holds me. How he loves me. And I feel guilty for causing any worry, for furrowing his brow. He is easy. I expect him. I know him. But I am tricky. One day here, the next day gone. He closes his eyes to disappointment. He utters the word "disappointment." And I bleed. He is all there is. I am broken.

I woke up today before sunrise to an ache in my soul. I stretched and pulled the covers close. I wanted to wish yesterday away, to make everything okay, the way he believes it is. I wanted to breathe in the here, the now. So I shed the crimson and the doubt. I went for a walk and breathed in the winter air.

Precarious. Life is precarious. Give and take. And sometimes it feels like a lot of take. Tonight he will hold me close and that is all. No before. No after. Mistakes will be forgiven. Secrets will remain silent. It will hold until another day when the flow will not stop and words must be spoken. For now it will rest. For now it is enough.

Let It Bleed

I take the X-Acto blade, press it into the flesh of my wrist, and pull. The blood forms a red line on my skin.

I exhale.

I move the blade, once used for fashion art projects, back to the beginning of the cut. I retrace, this time deeper. Wrist to elbow. Three inches. I do it again. And again.

I drop my hand down to the floor and the blood drips off my fingertips, crimson on the white linoleum. It is almost orgasmic. The voices in my head that demand blood grow quiet, replaced by a gentle hum.

That is enough. For now, that is enough.

The first time I wanted to cut my wrist I was a twenty-year-old junior in college. I wanted to be a fashion editor. I had dreams of something bigger and better than my small town, a town with not so much as a shopping mall. I had worked at W as a fashion intern the summer before. Once home I had fallen into a long, dark depression, so dark that this time, for the first time, I sought help. I went to the university counseling center and told them that my world was ending. They set up an appointment with the school's psychiatrist and she prescribed an antidepressant.

I took the pills religiously but still couldn't get up in the morning and once up couldn't go to bed early enough. Every morning my bedroom door would open a crack and there would be a moment of stillness.

"Good morning, sunshine," Brandon, my ex-boyfriend and roommate, always said, face pressed against the door frame.

"Why do you do that? Do I look sunshiney to you?" I said, angry to wake up to another day.

"Glad to see you're feeling peachy today," he said with a smile.

"Close my door, Brandon."

He told me months later when the sun reappeared that he did this every morning to check on me. He wanted to see that I was still breathing, that I was still alive. He lived in fear that I wouldn't make it through the dark days, the endless nights.

On a particular Saturday in November, morning gave way to afternoon and still I remained in my bed. Brandon came into my room and lay with me. We just breathed. I couldn't move my mouth to talk. It took too much energy.

I couldn't escape the feeling of despair. It surrounded me completely like the cold of that winter. And then there was this yearning, a yearning to cut myself open and let my pain bleed out of me. It didn't consume me, not yet. It simply suggested itself. One night I took my house key and pulled it across the delicate skin of my wrist. I did not bleed. It left only a red line from the metal on flesh. It was enough to scare me. I walked out of the house and wandered around campus for an hour until the urge lessened.

I was twenty-six when I finally gave in. I didn't want to feel pain. I was simply so consumed with the desire to cut that I could no longer fight it. It was an obsession. Cut yourself! Cut yourself! Cut yourself! Over and over my mind would demand blood and in the end, I couldn't take it any longer.

I cut late at night under the low illumination of the bathroom light. Sometimes I sat on the toilet in the bathroom of my tiny 425-square-foot apartment in Austin, Texas. Other times I sat on the floor in my panties and bra, cutting deeper and deeper until blood dripped off of my fingers, until I couldn't mop up the blood with paper towels and had to use the pale blue towels my mother bought me. I didn't feel pain. I only felt the relief that came, the quieting of voices in my head.

The bath water was blushing. I had cut my wrist and eased into the hot water. I had seen this in movies. I thought that the blood would come faster in the water. But then it was too much, sitting in a pool of my own blood. I pulled the towel off the rack and pressed it firmly on my wrist. When the bleeding lessened I stood up and dried off.

The next morning there was a blood-stained towel and red ring around the tub to remind me of what I had done.

Sex, drugs, rock and roll. Nothing in my life in the "Live Music Capital of the World" was as strong as my obsession to cut. I did so deeply and watched as the blood seeped from the split skin. Everything was silent—my apartment, my head. I traced the wound with the blade over and over again. Deeper. Deeper.

It was my twenty-seventh birthday and I sat that morning in yoga class. My wrist hurt as it stretched and flexed. I realized then that it had gone too far. The cuts had become too deep. At the end of class we sat, eyes closed, and breathed. Tears began to well beneath my closed eyelids and I surreptitiously wiped my cheeks. It was more than my wrist that was sore beneath the bandage; it was my soul.

That night there was a party, a gathering of my friends at a local bar to celebrate my birthday. A guy I had once dated picked me up with irises in hand. I wore a plum-colored tank top, a pale yellow, tiered-ruffle chiffon skirt—so short that if I bent over my nude lace panties would show—and sparkly bronze wedge sandals. He told me I looked good and I felt pretty in his gaze. I was thinner. I was working at the gym and had dropped the weight I'd gained at my last magazine job. We went to the bar and one by one my friends arrived until there was a sizeable group of fifteen or so. We sat beneath the late April stars, laughing and clinking glasses. I had no desire to cut; the only reason it crossed my mind was the constant ache in my wrist. I had told my best friend about the cutting and I pulled her aside to reveal the gash, peeling back the bandage.

"I called your mom," she said.

"You what?"

"I called your mom," she said. "I didn't know what else to do, Elaina."

And I was relieved. Help was on the way.

"Okay," I said. "I understand."

She gave me a big hug; she was good at that, wrapping her arms around me, making me feel safe.

From my bed the next morning I spoke with my mom.

"I'm going to come down there," she said.

"Ok," I said. "I think that's a good idea."

She didn't bring up the cutting and neither did I.

My mom arrived the next day. I saw her eyes flick towards my wrist. I flinched under her gaze. There was a bandage separating us. She came up to my apartment and settled in. She sat in my plush blue chair beneath the window.

"I need to go to the doctor's," I said.

"Why?"

"I cut myself and it's pretty bad."

"Let me see," she said gently.

I pulled back the bandage to expose the cut. I watched as she swallowed hard.

"You're right. Let's go to the doctor's."

I called the doctor's office and made an appointment for that afternoon. She drove me and I sat nervously in the front seat of her white PT Cruiser. When we got there I was self-conscious of my wrist, of what I'd done. Shortly after arriving I was called back into an exam room. I sat on the exam table looking at an illustration of the inner workings of an ear and waited for Dr. Bobby. I'd seen him before when I had bronchitis and I liked that he went by his first name. It made him honest and likeable. He came in wearing cowboy boots, jeans, and a plaid shirt with my chart in his hands.

"So, you have a cut?" he said and looked immediately to my wrist.

"Yes. I cut myself."

"Let's take a look," he said and I peeled away the bandage.

"That's a pretty bad cut, Elaina," he said. "Why did you do

this?"

I tried to find the words to explain it. I hadn't had to before and now I felt lost for words.

"I don't do it to hurt. It isn't for the reasons I've heard that others cut. It's like my mind gets obsessed with the thought. It tells me over and over again to cut and I get worn down until I can't fight any longer. It feels better to cut and silence my head than it does to fight the urge," I said.

"Well, you do need stitches, but you needed them yesterday. It's too late to do that now. You need to let this dry out. Keep it clean. Wash it a few times a day then dry it really well. Take the bandage off at night. I am going to put you on an antibiotic to be safe," he said.

He pulled back on his stool and looked me in the eye.

"You know, things get better," he said. "I know. There was a time when I was staring down the barrel of a gun. The gun was in my hand. I was tired of life. It was too hard. But as I stared at it, I realized something. I didn't want to die. I only wanted to stop feeling that way. So I put the gun down and cried. I cried for a long time. And it got better. Not all at once. Not overnight, but it got better. My life's not perfect, it never was. I meditate. I go on retreats. I take care of myself first. I'm telling you this because I want you to have hope. It isn't always going to be like this."

I looked at him, staring back into his brown eyes and nodded. I had no other words, so I thanked him—for taking care of my wound, for telling me his story. He left me in the room and a nurse came in and cleaned out my cut. She didn't ask me what happened. She didn't judge me. She smiled at me with a practiced compassion and applied a large bandage to my left wrist.

I went out to the waiting room when I was done. I paid the receptionist for my visit and held my prescription in hand. My mom was sitting there quietly waiting for me. We walked out to the car and as I took the passenger seat I began to cry.

"Don't cry, honey. It's going to be okay," she said and put her hand on my leg.

"I just feel so bad," I said. "I don't know what's wrong with me."

"The doctor came out to talk to me while you were in there. He said that if I wasn't here he would admit you to the hospital. He is worried about you."

I'd never been in the hospital before, not for anything other than a scheduled doctor's appointment. I was thankful for my mom and for this pardon.

During all this madness I dated Joe. He was tall with chestnut brown hair that touched his shoulders and celery green eyes. He'd been to New York to model but came back to Austin after breaking his nose. He worked on a television series as part of the crew. I met him at the gym where I worked. It started with a few words, then a few more, until eventually we were dating. Our conversations were deep and I relished the intimacy that came with them. One night as we sat on my gold antique couch he noticed the bandage on my wrist.

"Elaina. What happened to your wrist?" he asked.

"Oh, this? Nothing."

"Obviously something. What happened?"

"I don't want to talk about it," I said and leaned my head onto his shoulder.

I felt him sigh and squeeze my hand a little tighter.

On a lazy Saturday afternoon Joe and I went swimming in Barton Springs, a natural spring near downtown Austin. I wore a waterproof bandage and a lime green bikini. We lay on the grass and bathed in the sun. He told me I was beautiful and lying there in the late June sun I felt a stirring of some kind of happiness. When we sat in his forest green Jeep to leave he asked again about my wrist. I told him I'd cut it. He asked me why and I told him that I didn't know.

I decided to leave Austin that summer. My cousin, Kimberly, was having surgery on her spine back home in Oklahoma and I wanted to help her out. And as much as I wanted to help her, I knew that I, too, needed help. I needed support and love. The day three guys showed up to pack the contents of my apartment into the back of my dad's pickup truck and trailer, guys I'd dated and flirted with, I wore a large bandage that covered the inside of my left wrist. No one said anything about it. It was the elephant in my tiny apartment.

I hoped that things would get better, like Dr. Bobby had promised. But the cutting continued. It would abate long enough for the wounds to heal, sometimes days, sometimes months. My wrist became a mess of scars which I hid beneath large bracelets and watches worn face-in. A single small line adorned my right wrist and I had it tattooed as a deterrent for cutting. The line runs between the o and the v in "love." It is a reminder to love myself. I've considered tattooing the word "hope" on my left wrist so that when faced with the blade my wrist can offer it up.

I will be scarred for the rest of my life because of what I have done to myself. There was no accident. The thing out of control was me. Someday my twelve-year-old cousin will realize that I didn't scrape my wrist when I fell riding my bike, that instead I cut myself, that instead I wanted to die.

My illness is inside my mind, but my scars bring it out for the world to see. My scars say, See, something is wrong with me. I think the reason I cut is because it is my way of asking for help, of saying, I am hurt, please help me. I don't have the words to ask so I bleed.

I'd like to be able to write that I am done with it, that enough is enough. But I am mentally ill. My thoughts don't always make sense. Sometimes in my mania or depression I pick up a knife and carve. When it happens, after I have gone months without bleeding, I am ashamed because I always want to believe I am better. I want to believe that last time was the last time. I want to believe I am done with it. Moving on. Moving up.

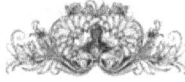

CHAPTER 6

Blog post

Once upon a time there was a girl who fell in love with a boy. He was a mean boy and would make her cry, make her crazy. But she was scared of him, too scared to leave him. Until one day, after an incident, she cut him off. He never left her life, always checking in on her, threatening her. Today, years later, he still checks up on her, reads her blog. He won't let her go.

What she learned most in that relationship was fear, how it felt, how it tasted in her mouth. She remembers the fighting and what it sometimes led to. And today she can still taste it in her mouth sometimes, that fear.

She avoids arguments, even disagreements, they scare her, make her think of him, of what he would say, what he would do. So when she lands in a disagreeable conversation or, heaven forbid, an argument, she wants to run. She wants to run far and fast. She wants to hide away.

They say time heals all wounds but I beg to differ. I was that girl who met a boy who changed my life. And if we don't agree on things—the shade of the grass, the smell of wet paint—I become scared of you. I pick up my feet and I run. I don't know what will change that. Will there come a day when I can hold fast to my opinion and feel safe?

Years have passed and I still worry about him finding me, about what he will do. I remember our fights, our awful fights, and it's these memories that shape my conversations, that make me tread lightly. I don't want to fight, not with anyone. It scares me too much. I'd rather stay quiet than risk it all again. Even love is not safe, he taught me that, love can hurt you.

The Spark

If you are bipolar, if it exists in your brain, it has always been there. You don't catch it like a nasty cold. It isn't a result of diet or exercise or lack thereof. It isn't from drinking too much or sleeping too little. It all has to do with the natural chemicals in your brain—too little, too much; it's still a mystery. It wasn't until I was in my late twenties that a psychiatrist sat on the other side of a large oak desk and said the words bipolar disorder. It is believed that stress can play a part in the onset of the illness. It may be the match to the flame of mental illness. Before my first manic episode, before the diagnosis, there was Ashton.

I met him in late 2003, at a Halloween party in Stillwater, Oklahoma, thrown by a mutual friend. He was dressed up as a soldier. He was Iranian American, born and raised in Alabama, with a Southern accent to prove it. His skin was like coffee with cream. His dark brown eyes were so dark it was hard to see the pupils and they were surrounded by thick, full lashes. I was twenty-two. He was nineteen. A week after the party we had a date. The week after that, another.

We dated for months. He was sweet and charming and I fell for him. Then one night I took him some peach cobbler I had made. I had spent the afternoon in the kitchen with my mother, cutting peaches, sifting flour. I took my time. For some reason, a reason I cannot remember, he became angry. He yelled at me and I got up to leave. I got as far as the door before he grabbed my bag, yanking me back into the apartment. He stood between me and the door, puffed up and big. Trapped, I sat on the couch as he told me what shit I was, what shit the cobbler was. I watched as he scraped the peaches into the trash. I began to cry as he cut me with his words. And then, as suddenly as he had begun, he stopped, came to me and apologized. I had made him mad. He didn't mean to scare me. He had picked me up from my parents' house in his Chevy and brought me to his apartment and eventually he took me home. I kissed him goodbye. Days later I noticed a bruise on my shoulder from where the strap of my bag had rubbed.

That was the beginning.

Our relationship went on in this pattern. He degraded me only to charm me back. There were roses and apologies, so many apologies. I fell in love with the good part of him, the part that made me smile and held me close. But I lived in shame. How could I let someone treat me the way he did and stay with him? Growing up I had sworn I would never be hurt by a boyfriend, but he never hit me. He shoved and pushed and grabbed, he left bruises, but didn't hit me. So I stayed. On the surface it shined. Two cute people in love. I was afraid to let anyone know what went on when it was just he and I. I was afraid of his violent temper.

One evening at his apartment while his roommate was away he became angry with me. Frightened, I scrambled to the bathroom to get away from him, but before I could close the door he flung it open. In an explosion he shoved me and I fell, my head missing the toilet by inches. With a look of shock on his face he helped me up and took me in his arms. He began to apologize.

"I almost hit my head on the toilet," I said in a small voice, afraid to ignite his temper.

"I didn't mean to make you fall, baby. You just made me so mad."

"You shouldn't have shoved me," I said.

"I didn't mean to. I'm sorry. Do you forgive me? Say you forgive me."

I stayed quiet, locked in his hug. He wasn't tall, only five foot seven, a few inches taller than me, but his anger was so big it made him bigger.

When I met him I was on a hiatus from New York. I had lived there for a year and returned home to Oklahoma while I looked for a permanent job back in the city. A few months after we started seeing each other I got a fashion assistant position at a start-up magazine in New York City. I left him behind in Oklahoma. He was prepared for me to leave, he knew I was trying to get back to New York, but he insisted we maintain our relationship. I figured some distance would do us good. There was less time to anger him during visits. I hoped for a change.

One afternoon I was sitting at my desk in Manhattan working on procuring some garments for an upcoming photo shoot at the fashion magazine. It was a cool spring day, the kind that hints of warmer weather and begins to wave goodbye to winter.

"Surprise!" I heard from behind a dozen red roses. I loved the lightest shade of pink, a pink that appears as though a white rose is blushing. He always bought me red.

He pulled the roses away from his face and beamed. I wasn't expecting him, not in New York, not at my work. But I was happy to see him. I introduced him to my boss, who gave me the afternoon off to spend with Ashton. The days he stayed were a whirlwind of romance. He took me to dinners and kissed me on the street. He never raised his voice or his hand. It reminded me of the reason why I was so drawn to him and when he left, I missed him.

After nine months in New York I returned to my parents' home in Oklahoma. I was done with New York and its frantic pace. I wanted to slow down and enjoy life. I was ready for a break. Ashton was excited for my return and the opportunity to be closer to me.

On New Year's Eve of 2004 we hung out during the day, fighting. He wanted to go out that night but I didn't want to be around him. He insisted we ring in the New Year together and showed up at my house that evening. I didn't want to explain to my parents why I didn't want to go out, to explain that anything was wrong, so I went with him. As soon as I was in the car he started.

"You don't deserve me," he said. "I do everything for you and you don't even care. You are a college graduate who can't even get a fucking job for shit. Are your parents proud? You talk about OSU and what are you doing now?" He laughed. "So you went to New York, who the fuck cares? Look at you now."

He called a friend back home in Alabama.

"My girlfriend is being a bitch," he said. "Yeah, I am still with her...I know, hopefully not for long."

I sat quietly in the passenger seat. I was scared and just wanted to get out of the car, to get away from him. He got off the phone, threw me a dirty look, and pulled into the parking lot in downtown Oklahoma City. I took off my jacket and we got out of the car. As we began to walk he tried to hold my hand but

I didn't want to take his. Then he picked me up and carried me back to the car. I was afraid of what he would do to me so I kicked him hard. I began to plead with him to put me down. He told me he was afraid I would leave him there in Oklahoma City in the crowd if he let me go, but I promised not to. I told him I had left my favorite red leather motorcycle jacket in the car and wouldn't abandon it. We walked around downtown and we ran into my sister and her friends. I didn't say anything about Ashton, didn't ask for help. My pride got in the way and I walked away from her with Ashton.

The night was without pleasure. We stood beneath the fire-works and kissed at midnight. We got back into the car. Driving home, he once again began his litany of apologies. He pulled over on the side of the highway and there in the dark tried to make me understand that it was my fault he had acted the way he did. It was always my fault.

We turned off the highway onto the dark country road that led to my home. As he apologized I stayed quiet. We passed my gravel road and headed into an empty gas station parking lot. As he spoke I got a piece of gum out of my purse. I was so tired of him and the endless sound of his voice telling me it was always my fault. I just wanted to make it stop. I balled up the wrapper of my gum and tossed it in his face. He reached over and grabbed me by my curly brown hair on each side of my head and shook me, my whole body. Back and forth for endless moments. Scared, I opened the car door and tried to get out but he quickly gunned the gas and I pulled the door closed. He jerked out of the parking lot and back onto the dark road. We began to speed. He reached over me. He opened the passenger door. He tried to shove me out of the moving car. I saw the ditch covered in grass. I felt the cold January wind whip my hair into my face. I held on to the console with my left hand with an adrenaline surge of strength. He re-turned his hand to the steering wheel as we flew over a hill in the night. I pulled the door closed. I could taste the fear, metallic on my tongue. I wanted to disappear, to be anywhere, anywhere, but sitting in that car with a man who could kill me. Despite my-self, I began to cry. Suddenly he slowed down, then turned the car around in the direction of my road. He began his apologies. He begged for forgiveness. He tried to touch me and I winced.

When we finally pulled into my driveway I jumped from the car. I ran around the back of the Chevy and through the chain link gate to the red front door. I was shaking so hard I dropped my keys. My heart stopped as I bent to pick them up. I heard him open his car door. I carefully, quickly, slid the key into the lock, turned it, slid through the door and locked it behind me. The house was quiet as my parents slept. I walked into the bathroom and locked the door and lay down on the cool pink tiles and cried until the shaking stopped.

The next day I told my parents I didn't want to see or talk to him but I didn't tell them why. I was too embarrassed. I felt like it was my fault for being in a relationship with someone who treated me the way he did. I had made the choice. I had to deal with the consequences.

When Ashton came to the door with a letter, my father told him I didn't want to see him. My father took the letter and then handed it to me after he had closed the door. In the letter Ashton promised to attend anger management classes. He promised that it would never happen again. His list of apologies went on for two pages.

I didn't talk to Ashton for a month and a half, and then one day he showed up at my door with flowers and a part of me, the part that believed in the good in him, gave him that Valentine's Day to make me smile again, and he did. Part of me was scared of him, of what had happened and what he might do to me if I rejected him, so we got back together, my fear of him so great.

A month later I got a job in Austin, Texas. I had decided while living in New York that Austin was my next stop. I had heard great things about the city and was excited to slow down. I pestered the publisher of a local lifestyle magazine until he gave me a job as an assistant editor.

I hoped that the distance between Ashton and me would be enough to end things. I hoped he would get tired of me and move on to someone new. Within a month of moving I broke things off with him. I'd had enough and I felt safe that I was far enough away to escape his wrath.

One day shortly after the break-up, my boss called me into his office and told me that Ashton had called him to find out if I was free for the upcoming weekend. My boss had told him that it wasn't his place to discuss my personal life and that it was something Ashton should contact me about. My boss warned me to not let my personal life affect my job and, embarrassed, I left his office. That night I called Ashton and told him I wanted him out of my life completely. I valued my career. I had worked so hard to get to where I was. He had crossed a line and there was no going back.

A few days later he showed up at my door, having driven seven hours from his new home in Mississippi. At first he was kind as he stood in my doorway, pleading with me to take him back. But when he realized that his words had lost their pull, he grew irritated. He demanded that I return the stuff he had given to me during our relationship. I agreed to get the things and tried to shut the door. He put his foot inside and kept it from closing. He told me he wanted to keep the door open so that I wouldn't shut him out. Reluctantly I turned my back and in seconds he was inside. I asked him to leave but there was something burning in his eyes. He grabbed me and slammed me against the wall. Through gritted teeth he told me how worthless I was, how I would never find someone to love me again. He told me the only things he missed were my tits and that was all anyone noticed about me, that without them I was nothing. Then he threw me onto the couch. This time I did not freeze in fear, I knew my escape was just beyond the door eight feet away. Eight feet from the couch to the front door. All I had to do was convince him.

"Let's go for a walk," I suggested.

"No. If we go outside you will run away," he countered.

"No, I won't. I promise. I just don't want to stay in here. Let's go for a walk."

"You will run away," he said.

"I won't," I promised.

We left the apartment and headed out to the sidewalk. We walked across the street to the local grocery store. I sat down in the parking lot. I would not get up.

"My mom and sister are on their way here," I told him.

"No, they aren't."

"They are. I promise," I said. "You should leave."

To prove that they were coming for a visit planned a month before I called my mom on my cell phone and kept her on speaker phone. I asked her how far away she was and when I could expect her.

"Fine," he said after I ended the call. "I'll go, but I want my stuff back."

"I will send it to you in the mail," I said.

He squatted down and kissed me on the cheek. I watched him walk away and didn't leave that spot in the parking lot until I saw his car pull out.

It was shortly after his visit that the harassment began. He would send me pages of callous words. His anger was just as ugly on paper as it had been in person.

You just bring out the worst in me. It actually feels good to be a jerk to you because you are such a deserving bitch....The fact is that you are a stubborn, pigheaded bitch and the fact is that your fake and stuck-up personality makes me want to vomit!...But that is why people screw you over, because you lead them on and mess with their heads and fill them with false hope and lie to them.

Then he began to call me at work. Our office had only one number, so I could not screen my calls. On the phone he would threaten me. He vowed to tell my boss that I was an alcoholic or a thief, whatever he could say to tarnish my reputation, to plant the seeds of doubt. He wrote letters to my parents and my best friend. He somehow got the numbers of my ex-boyfriends and called them to tell them nasty things about me. His mouth was a lie.

After speaking to Ashton, my ex-boyfriend Brandon called me.

"Be careful," he warned. "I'm a big guy and I'm scared of him."

"What can I do?" I asked. Ashton had all the control and I was at his mercy.

"Get a baseball bat. Something. I'm scared for you, Elaina."

One day, a month later, I noticed a car from Alabama in my parking lot. I couldn't see the driver. Scared, I called a friend and made plans to stay with her. We went out to eat and I told her all about the situation with Ashton. She called her friend who was a lawyer and I talked to him. He told me that what was happening was called harassment and I should go to the police.

I made an appointment with a detective at the Austin Police Department and visited her downtown. She was feminine and quick and within a few minutes we were sitting in uncomfortable chairs across from each other at a table. I told her what had happened so far and shared the letters Ashton had sent to me. I was humiliated to have anyone read the crude and sexual words. Because Ashton was in the military she promised to call his command. Perhaps that would stop his behavior. We made an appointment to meet the following week.

I didn't respond to Ashton when he wrote and emailed. I sat uncomfortably at Seattle's Best coffee shop and told my boss that my ex-boyfriend was harassing me just as the detective had advised me to do. I explained the threats over my latte and watched the concern in his eyes grow. I went back to see the detective and she told me that she had contacted his command and had been told that Ashton had said that I was a troublemaker and would probably try to cause problems for him. He was smart, covering his bases in advance. The detective had spoken to him and told him to leave me alone.

He couldn't be arrested for what he was doing but if he showed up at my door I could call the police and have him arrested for stalking—a felony. I hoped it wouldn't come to that. His emails became fewer and fewer and the calls to my work stopped.

One night, at a bar in Austin, I saw him. I was dancing with my best friend when he caught my eye. I looked to her and saw that she recognized him too. I had been checking his MySpace page from time to time to keep tabs on him, to make sure he was far away from me, and knew he was living in Alabama. I watched as minutes later he left the bar. I spent that night at my girlfriend's apartment in case he came looking for me, even though I was living in a new place. The next day I talked to the drummer in the band that had played at the bar—a friend of mine. He told me that Ashton had warned the guys via MySpace that I was a "hit-it and quit-it" girl. He told me that Ashton had claimed to be a booker for a club in Alabama. I knew he wasn't a booker. I knew how Ashton could manipulate people, tell them what they wanted to hear. I knew he showed up because he had seen my post telling the band I would be at the show. He was watching me. Still.

He would pop up every few months—send an email, call my

cell phone, even though I had changed the number. He told me he knew people, people who could get him any information he wanted. That I could not hide from him. He would wait just long enough for me to think it was over and then he would sneak back into my life. I never let down my guard. Because of his violent temper I was always afraid of what he might do to me, how he might hurt me.

My fear began to manifest itself as anxiety. I couldn't go to the grocery store because I was afraid he was there in the next aisle, waiting for me. I couldn't enjoy Austin's nightlife because in a dark crowd I worried he would show up, like he had done before. I started having panic attacks. I would sweat and shake and lose my breath. At a bar I hid in a bathroom stall waiting for my heart to stop racing. Every dark-haired stranger was him. I felt like I was going to die.

I changed my phone number a few times over the next six years in an effort to hide from him. I made sure to never mention where I was in any of my blogs or internet posts and asked my friends and family to do the same. Six years after our relationship ended his interest in me and my life remained. He read my blog—him, or someone else I didn't know with an IP address in Tuscaloosa, Alabama, where he was in school. He never stopped watching me and my fear of him has never gone away. If he could be so dangerous when he loved me, what is he capable of now?

I don't blame my bipolar disorder on Ashton. It doesn't work that way. I think the stress he caused me—over such a long period of time—wore me down. He was the match that lit the fire of my bipolar disorder. After the anxiety started I was engulfed—depression, cutting, an eventual suicide attempt. He was a match and he set me ablaze.

CHAPTER 7

Blog post

I recently had a conversation with someone who argued that everyone has, to an extent, obsessive compulsive disorder (OCD). I understood his point. We all have our quirks. Some must use a new cup each time they get a new beverage; others must alphabetize their library collection. There are many things people must do—only write in blue ink, brush their teeth for a certain length of time, do laundry on Sunday. I get it, everyone has their thing.

I have obsessive compulsive disorder—I have been diagnosed by psychiatrists and psychologists. It's not something I simply believe or have self-diagnosed. It is not a quirk or two. So what does that mean? We've all heard about it and seen it on T.V. For me it affects my life on a daily basis. It is very real for some of us and to make light of it is uncomfortable.

My family and my boyfriend help me. They do not enable me but rather help me to function. They try to help me see logically though it is usually in vain. Mental illnesses are not something one chooses or can simply turn off. They are like a broken brain, bad wiring.

Obsessed

One-two-three-four-five-six-seven-eight-nine-ten. One-two-three-four-five-six-seven-eight-nine-ten. If I can just keep counting everything will be okay. Over and over again. And over again. One-two-three-four-five-six-seven-eight-nine-ten. I want the numbers to make it stop, to make it better. I want to feel them wash over me like a digital baptism. They come fast, I breathe them in. I breathe them out. I close my eyes and see them falling—so fast, trying to keep up with my pace. One-two-three-four-five-six-seven-eight-nine-ten. My breath is short and fast and chops the air. The numbers run past my lips softly, as if afraid to be heard, afraid of being real. One-two-three-four-five-six-seven-eight-nine-ten. My lips move but no one can hear me. Please, don't let anyone hear me. Nails dig into my palms. I swallow a pill, tiny and peach. I count the seconds until it works. One-two-three-four-five-six-seven-eight-nine-ten.   One-two-three-four-five-six-seven-eight-nine-ten. I count my heartbeats. I want to run away; I want to count my steps. I feel fear receding as the numbers slow down. Their sprint becomes a trot, becomes a walk. Ingested, they meander through my body, through my veins. Everything will be okay. Everything will be okay.

It began with numbers when I was twenty-seven years old, even digits safe, odds a danger. The volume dial on the radio has to be set to an even number. The television follows shortly after. I can't sit still with an odd number in the room. It looms like a dark cloud above my head, raining its poison over me. My family learns of the quirk and accommodates me.

"She likes the even numbers. No problem."

And so it begins, the obsession with numbers.

I look at the clock. 3:57. I look again. 3:59. It's bad luck. I catch the numbers like butterflies in a net, butterflies that turn into crows. These black omens of death flap their wings in an effort to free themselves from the tangled strings. Check the clock again. 4:01. The number pricks my flesh, claws piercing my skin. My eyes fight the desire to look again at the clock on the car radio, not wanting to catch another bird. 4:02. I catch my breath, I rest on the two, slide down its curved back. Breathe it in, black feathers on the wind. At 4:03 I begin to count. One-two-three-four-five-six-seven-eight-nine-ten.   One-two-three-four-five-six-seven-eight-nine-ten. I need to make the numbers behave, stop this flock of birds from picking my skin from bones. I cannot control them.

Knees drawn up to my chest, I perch on a blue upholstered chair. The waiting area is small. Chairs around a coffee table. Magazines from four months ago. End tables with pamphlets offering up mental illness like a menu with nothing good to eat. The windows look out over the campus of Duke University. It's a rainy fall day and the street lights have just come on. The few people outside rush from building to building. Duke is supposed to be one of the best. I am paying them to fix me. I've come out of a meeting with other broken people. In the middle of the psychobabble the fear crept over me and I fled.

The carpet is deep blue with a terra-cotta colored pattern, diamonds in the sky. I count the floor. Each diamond, every diamond. There are thirty-seven. I need there to be thirty-eight, so I start again, only to end up where I began. I get up off the chair and walk away from it and the others and the wooden tables. I leave the magazines behind like yesterday's news. One-two-three-four-five....Each step gets a number and its heel to toe, heel to toe. I pace down the length of the hall and back again. I can't stop. I wish away anyone from finding me like this: a girl stuck in her steps.

I can't get out of bed. I wait for the clock to tell me it is safe, an even number to reassure me. I pull the covers up, afraid of the illuminated seven. It's safe here in my bed, the place I come for comfort. When the numbers won't stop or I am afraid, I run to my bed. It holds me to the Earth. It keeps me from flying into the sky. On it, on me, rests a quilt my mother made me for college graduation. Blue kimonos celebrating Japan, the place I was born. In the corner is stitched, I love you. I'm afraid to watch the alarm clock, afraid of the lucky dice. I look at the eight blinking back at me. I pull the covers off in one sweeping motion and hurry my feet to the floor, watching the clock. I can't get stuck in a nine.

Twenty-five. I have washed my hands twenty-five times and I can't stop. I feel the hot water as it burns at my skin. I pump the soap. Each finger gets a turn. I start with my thumb, then hold my right index finger in my left fist. Up and down. I scrub it...then the middle finger, then my ring finger, then my pinky. I scour my nails above and below. I wash my wrist and my palm. I lather the back of my hand. Then I turn to the left hand. The ritual repeats. Up and down. Above and below. Around and around. I hold my hands beneath the burning water, left knob cranked. My hands are red and splotchy but I can't get them clean. Twenty-six. Every moment I do this I feel more out of control. I've just touched a dirty washcloth. It fell on the floor and I had to pick it up. If only I could leave it there, soiled on the floor. The germs on the rag have contaminated my fingers, my hand, my body. I will never be clean.

I'm walking in Walmart. I pass the aisles overflowing with cold medicine and flu remedies. DayQuil. NyQuil. Sudafed. I feel something brush my left elbow. She passes me, unaware of what she has just done. The dark hair of a short woman has touched my arm, hair that cascades down her back to her waist. Too long. Too long. The dead cells, the germs they harbor have been transferred to me. Her hair is dirty, I know this without knowing whether she washed it this morning. I know this in my heart.

I'm at the bar with my boyfriend. It's called Blackwater Grille, though it sits near no water and has closed the restaurant a few months ago. I sit on a high wooden stool and he stands next to me, hands on my thighs. I'm wrapped up in the words coming from his perfect lips. His mouth is a welcome mat to my home. The music is loud in here. I feel it. The crowd is thick with girls in short dresses and guys in button-down shirts. I sit up straight. I feel something at my right elbow and turn around. Her hair trails down her back like my nightmare, long and blonde. I turn back to my boyfriend.

"What's wrong?" he asks.

"Her hair," I answer. He looks over my shoulder and sees her.

"Don't worry about it, baby. You are okay," he says but I can't hear him. All I can hear is the voice in my head, the one telling me she's dirty, telling me I'm dirty. He rubs my thighs and looks into my eyes.

"You're okay, baby." But I'm not. Tears contort the room. I won't cry, but I want to. The polished wood of the bar has become a frenzy of germs and I can no longer rest my elbows on it. I hold my arms awkwardly in front of me as though I am about to box, as though I will knock her out cold. I want to be clean. I don't want to feel this way. I want to be anyone but me.

At this meeting with my therapist I stare down at the chair, offended. I do not see black cloth on metal, I see germs. Millions. I debate my options. I reach in my bag and pull out a tiny bottle of Lysol and spray the chair, a magic wand vanquishing what is visible only to my eyes. She notices me, my hand, my fear.

"What are you doing?" she asks.

"The chair is dirty," I reply.

"Is that why you sprayed the chair?" she asks in the way therapists ask seemingly redundant questions.

"Yes," I tell her, "I can't sit on it like this, too many germs."

I perch on the chair, afraid of contact—skin to fabric, clothing not enough of a barrier. My legs before me form a perfect upside down L with the floor. My back is stiff and straight and points to the ceiling. She sits back in her chair, comfortable in it, in her own skin. My own skin crawls. How can she do that? Doesn't she feel it? Doesn't she worry? She watches me and I know how this must seem. I feel two parts of me fight. One side rationally knows that what germs there are will not hurt me. The other side fears them, fears what they will do to me, fears being unclean. The fear wins.

I reach up in the cupboard and pull down a glass. Spotless. I smell it and then rinse it out. Count to three. I do this every time I drink. I do it at home. I do it at my grandmother's. I'm at a Halloween party and I open cupboards looking for the cups. When I find them I choose one. I look over it then look around. No one is watching, I surreptitiously put my nose to the vessel. I sniff then reach out for the faucet. I need to know it's clean and somehow this ritual makes it okay. I cannot drink any other way. Sniff and rinse. Sniff and rinse. There is no other way.

The numbers are getting worse. The even ones are no longer safe, it is only multiples of five that give me comfort. In my boyfriend's car he turns the volume to fifteen, then to twenty without looking at me. I'm not afraid to tell him about this, that I can only sit still with a five or a zero trailing a number. He tells me he loves me.

I'm watching television with my parents and my dad forgets. He turns up the volume so we can better hear the actor reciting his lines. Twenty-eight. I tell myself it is okay, that it's just a number, that everything will be okay, but it isn't. I wait until the commercial break and casually get up. I walk up the stairs. Left, right, left, right. I walk into the bathroom and close the door and turn the left knob only. Then, I wash my hands. Over and over again.

We walk up to the door at Outback Steakhouse. I pause before the door waiting for my boyfriend to open it. I cannot touch the handle. All the hands that have come before me have touched it, hands not washed, hands that cover a cough, a sneeze. Dirty hands.

"How many?"

"Two.

"Right this way, please."

We sit down in a booth to the right of the room. The seats are red leather or a fabric that pretends to be leather. The restaurant is dim this evening, but the light above our table illuminates the paper coasters. We sit side by side on one side of the booth as though we are waiting for someone to join us. He opens the menu and holds it for me. They don't wash the menus like they wash down the tables. Only I realize how dirty this is, only I can count the germs. I look it over, choosing a salad. Our waiter, Rob, comes. He squats next to our table. He is young, just out of high school. His brown hair falls over his left eye and he constantly shakes his head to clear his view. He walks away and I unwrap my silverware. There is a spot of food on the fork. My boyfriend switches with me until we can exchange it. And suddenly it is too noisy in the restaurant and there are too many people. I can't breathe.

"I have to go outside," I say as I scoot him out of the booth.

"Okay. Do you want me to come with you?" he asks.

"No. You stay with our table," I say. "I need to get out."

I walk through the double doors and sit down on a wooden bench. I take a deep breath in and start to count. One-two-three-four-five-six-seven-eight-nine-ten. One-two-three-four-five-six-seven-eight-nine-ten. I count until my head stops spinning, until my breathing slows. I count all the things that are wrong as I wish for things to be made right. People walking into the restaurant look at me. Up and down. What do they see? A woman on the brink? A woman talking to herself? A woman alone.

It's the first day of graduate school and taciturn is stuck in my head. It goes round and round like dirty clothes in a washing machine. I stand beneath the warm shower. Taciturn. My hands go up to my head and rub in the shampoo until tiny bubbles form on my hair. Taciturn. I try to think of something else, my first class, my long commute to Wilmington, but the letters stick to my brain like wet clothes on the floor. I put the garments on, they cling to my skin—my breasts, my thighs. I stand beneath the water and feel its warmth on my head, the bubbles run smooth. Taciturn.

I scratch the back of my hand. I must have been doing it for some time because it is raw, the skin peeled back from the wound. Back and forth I move my nail across my skin, deeper and faster. I've just shaken my new therapist's hand, warm skin to cool. Her fingers wrapped around mine like a vise. I feel the contamination of my skin, the dirty that will never be clean. There are scabs on my hands, moments like this. They will leave scars that linger, small dark patches like a series of birthmarks. They will leave memories.

I open the medicine cabinet and feel something catch in my throat. I turn each bottle and tube towards me, soldiers forming a precise line. I pull each item to the edge of the shelf, making sure it is even with the others. That's better. That's better. Later I get the ketchup out of the fridge and close the door. Seconds tick by and I must open it again and rearrange everything, all labels must face front. I turn the relish; I turn the butter. That evening I lift a laundered towel off the bed. I fold it once, corners lining up perfectly. I fold it again and again. When I'm done I examine the edges. Not right. Not right. I shake out the towel and start again. It needs to be perfect. I need to be perfect.

OCD. Three tiny letters, not much to count. Obsessive compulsive disorder. I've been treated, not cured. There is no magic pill, only a wrong I cannot make right. There are only germs and numbers and the feel of my skin. One-two-three-four-five-six-seven-eight-nine-ten. There are only spinning words and uneven bottles. There are only clean hands and dirty looks. There aren't enough stars in the sky to wish this away. There isn't enough air in the room. One-two-three-four-five-six-seven-eight-nine-ten. One-two-three-four-five-six-seven-eight-nine-ten.

It's a nightmare I wake up to and fall asleep with every night. I want to be different. I want to be you. I want to reach out and pull open the door. Twist the knob, feel the cool metal in my palm. I want to borrow your pen and hold it between my fingers without wanting to run away. I want to sip from my boyfriend's straw, taste the sweet syrup, let the bubbles dance upon my tongue. I want to put away the hand sanitizer, the portable Lysol, the worries that haunt me. I want to rest my fork upon the table, to rest my mind for a while. I want to wash my hands just once, only once, and forget how good it feels to rinse and repeat. I want to be unburdened. I want my skin to be free of these scars, my memory wiped clean. I want the numbers to leave me alone, to fly once more from my lips up higher, higher, with the butterflies and the crows.

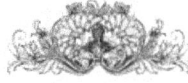

CHAPTER 8

Blog post

The truth

Last year I applied to graduate school to obtain a Masters of Fine Arts in Creative Writing. I wanted to study fiction, I want to write books. I sent applications and two short stories (thirty pages of writing) to a handful of schools coast to coast. I was accepted to and excited about attending The School of the Art Institute of Chicago. Not quite ready, I deferred for a year and am set to go this upcoming fall. I had very much wanted to get into the University of North Carolina at Wilmington; it's a 1% school—meaning only that many of the applicants get in. I was not one of the six. I decided to try again this year. Heck, I've already been rejected—why not? Instead of focusing on fiction I would put my energy into something closer to home—the truth. I'm finding it is easier to write when there are facts and opinions and an already existent personality. I've been a journalist for years now; perhaps this is the next step, perhaps it makes more sense. My practice and experience lies in sharing stories, true stories. So I am trying it again, rustling up another manuscript, this time of things that were and are, not of what I imagine them to be. Maybe the truth will write itself.

The Next Step

As the darkness began to lift ever so slightly months after my suicide attempt, I looked to the future with trepidation. Would I ever be well again? When would I be able to work? What about living on my own; what would I do with myself? I could no longer see who I wanted to be, and who I had been was now gone. I thought again about what I loved just as I had as a senior in high school a decade before. What was I good at? And I realized that in all my jobs, I had loved writing the most. I loved creating something from nothing, telling a story. So I decided that I would apply to graduate school to study creative writing. I wouldn't have to leave until late summer and I hoped to be well enough, strong enough, brave enough to go by then.

I applied to several schools around the country that focus on the study of fiction. I was accepted into The School of the Art Institute of Chicago. I was excited about the opportunity, but hesitant to make a move so far away from my family. As enrollment got closer I knew I wasn't ready to leave my support system, so I deferred for a year.

I had also applied to the University of North Carolina Wilmington to study fiction, just as I had at the Chicago school, and was unpleasantly rejected. Now I had another year to think and prepare for graduate school. I realized that maybe fiction wasn't quite right for me. I had always written personal essays for magazines and websites; perhaps I should study creative nonfiction. I applied again to UNCW, but this time I applied for the creative nonfiction program, one of the top in the country. I submitted a single essay, a version of the first chapter of this book. Months crawled by as I waited for a letter telling me if I was in or I was out. I got in and told The School of the Art Institute of Chicago that I would not be attending in the fall.

Before I knew it, it was the summer of 2010. I had been living in North Carolina for almost a year with my parents and was excited that the university was just an hour and a half away from their house. Unlike Chicago, if I needed them, they were just a short drive away. My parents and I went apartment hunting for a place that would accommodate my eighty-five-pound dog. We found a place with a pool and dog park and two bedrooms on the top floor of the building. My brother, dad, mom, and I carried all my boxes and furniture up flights of stairs just as graduate school started.

Before I enrolled in classes I went through the process of applying for disabled status. I worried about what would happen if I had a bipolar episode. The school granted me disabled status and I met with each of my professors in private and told them I had a disability that might limit me from attending classes at times. They were concerned and kind and I felt a little relief.

Before school ever began I was matched up with a mentor—someone already in the Master of Fine Arts program who would answer my questions and help guide me in this new land of literature. Her name was Brandy, and from the pictures I saw posted on her profile she was a striking redhead. I asked her about taking two workshops at once, something that wasn't recommended for a first-year student. I asked her about how many people tended to fill a class. And then one day, when she asked what I wanted to write about, I told her I wanted to write about what it was like to have bipolar disorder.

"Oh. Listen. I have to run to the grocery store."

"Um, okay," I said.

She never mentored me after that. This was what I consider my first taste of prejudice, of stigma, of finding someone who believed that people with mental illness are worth less than those without. And it hurt. And it made me never want to tell anyone again, to never say the words "bipolar disorder" or "depression" or "anxiety" or "OCD." It made me never want to say those words, but it didn't stop me from opening my mouth.

I had just three classes—a reading- and discussion-based class, a fiction workshop, and a nonfiction workshop. I looked the part of a creative writer in my flirty little dresses and high wedges, carrying my notebooks and pens, but I felt entirely out of my league. Most of my classmates came with English or undergraduate writing degrees. I had only ever taken one English composition class required at Oklahoma State University. I didn't know the literary terms they threw around so easily like jocks threw footballs. For them it seemed so easy.

Workshops were a new thing for me. My fiction professor

required each student to write two stories to be shared with the class. We were then required to read and respond to the story by writing a letter to the author. I enjoyed reading the stories of these talented writers, but found the letter-writing challenging. I am an avid reader but had never had to critique someone else's work.

My nonfiction workshop was an entirely different beast and I loved it. We did some readings. We went on a field trip to a park to help us understand how to write about a place, how to make it a character of a story. We had shorter writing assignments, which were never graded, but if we wanted, the professor would read them and respond to us individually. We wrote one longer piece that we workshopped. I wrote a version of what is the OCD chapter of this book. I felt so much stronger writing creative nonfiction than fiction. Maybe because it was real, maybe because it was something I needed to share, to get out, to tell the world.

My apartment was big enough for me and my dog, though I know she must have longed for a yard instead of leashed walks. My mom and I painted my office a pale blue. I filled up the closets in both rooms with my clothes and handbags and shoes. I ate dinner alone at a 1950s yellow and chrome table that had belonged to my great-grandmother. I had my reading chair set next to a lamp-topped table in the corner of the living room where I spent my evenings reading. When the weather was nice my dog and I would sit out on the balcony of our third-story apartment. I would do my homework and she would lie and watch the coming and going of the other residents.

My mom came to visit. We went for coffee and ordered pizza and watched movies. My dad came and went fishing while I was in class. My boyfriend, Jeremy, came for a wonderful week. But in their absence I was lonely. I tried to make friends but my social anxiety made it tough. I wasn't drinking so I took bottled iced tea to the few parties I was invited to, which perhaps only added to my weirdness.

My anxiety caused my obsessive compulsive disorder to get worse. I started washing my hands over and over again. I would wash them twenty-five, thirty, thirty-five times before I could leave the apartment to go to class. I started lining things up. You could read every label in the fridge when you opened the door because I lined them all up that way. Every item in the medicine cabinet had its place and was pulled precisely to the edge of the shelf. My closets were still color coordinated. I just felt like if things weren't just so, just perfect, then everything would crumble to pieces.

I did find a friend in Sandy. She also dealt with anxiety. She was my age, a good five years older than our classmates. We lamented about how we would surely fail out of graduate school, how we weren't good enough, or smart enough, or as talented as the rest of them.

But the secret was—we were. I finished the semester with all As and comments from my workshopped pieces confirmed that I was, in fact, talented. My amazing peers saw it, as did my impressive professors. It seemed that I was the only one who was having trouble believing it.

By the end of the semester in December I was so stressed and anxious and lonely I decided to take a leave of absence. I wanted some time to decide if I should return. So I recruited a few guys to help me move back out and briefly went back to my parents' house. In January I moved to Virginia to live with Jeremy. As time went on I felt confident in my decision not to go back to UNCW and notified them that I would not be returning.

I never felt like I failed for only attending one semester of graduate school. I felt proud that I had been strong enough to live on my own again outside the watchful eyes of my parents. It gave me back some of the trust in myself that I had lost after I tried to kill myself. I felt proud that I had made it.

CHAPTER 9

Blog post

I don't have a lot to report from here. I'm not out partying like my former rockstar self (but oh when I do…), I'm not fluttering around as social butterflies are apt to do. My universe has become much smaller, a greenhouse as opposed to the open fields. And that's just the way it is…for now.

I have a new puppy. As a Bernese Mountain Dog, she's, well, big boned. Not even four months old, she weighed in last week at 32lbs. She should get up to 80, I think. I've wanted a dog for years, after losing my collie, Freedom, in 2004;I was ready but unable because of apartment restrictions. I got her in December and she's hilarious. She's big and bold and so very vain, often checking herself out in mirrors. She's a princess and sleeps on a pink fuzzy pillow known as "Princess Pillow."When she leaves her crate in the morning, she won't leave without Princess Pillow in her mouth. It's like her security blanket. Quite cute. We've started puppy class. I plan to take her through obedience classes until she can become a therapy dog. I'd like to be able to take her into children's hospitals and cheer them up with a big furry beast.

Finding a Purpose

When you are depressed you need a reason to go on, because you are not enough. You desire death like a hungry child standing outside a bakery window. You are consumed by it. You lie in bed and think of ways to die. You concentrate on the prescription pills waiting on your nightstand, joined by a glass of room-temperature water. You think about the knife you keep under the bathroom sink, the ones on the kitchen counter. You think of these ways because these are the ways you have tried to hurt yourself before.

And you nearly succeeded in dying.

You won't answer your cell phone anymore. Hell, you won't even charge it. Your blog will grow idle. There will be no words because your words are now gone. They drifted away with your mind. Slowly. Imperceptibly.

Your mother will worry. She will fuss over you the way she did when you were a newborn and wouldn't stop crying in the night. She will cook your favorite meals; food you will not eat. She will lose sleep. At night you will wake to a crack of light and her silhouette standing in the doorway of the guest bedroom that is now your room. She will try to get you to go to a movie, go for a walk, go for a cup of coffee—just get you out of the house. She thinks fresh air will do you good, that sun on your pale face will cheer you up.

Your parents offer to buy you a puppy. You waver. How can you take care of a puppy when you cannot take care of yourself?

You research breeds. Study books. Peruse the Internet. You decide on a Bernese Mountain Dog. You find a breeder in the state and contact her. Yes, she has a litter. Yes, she has a female. They were born on October 8th. That is the day you were released from the hospital after you tried to kill yourself. You see this as a sign.

It's early December. Your mother drives you to Oklahoma City, where you wait in the parking lot of Bass Pro Shops. You don't drive anymore. They won't let you. They don't trust you. You are still fragile. You still dream of death and they don't want to give you a vehicle to kill yourself in. It is a cold day, gray, like it is going to rain.

A black minivan pulls up beside you. The woman in the passenger seat waves. Everyone gets out. Your mother hands over a check and they open the trunk. There, in a dog crate, is your puppy. She is bigger than you expected and you notice her large feet. The woman opens the crate door and scoops her up. The woman turns her body and hands you the puppy. The black and brown and white fur is warm and you kiss the dog's head.

"What are you going to name her?" the woman asks.

"Hope."

A month later we head to her first obedience class. Once a week my parents drive me to Oklahoma City's Armory. They bring chairs and drinks and sit and watch as Hope and I practice basic commands like heel, sit, and wait. I laugh as Hope nervously encounters her first staircase and climbs it. The building is dark and there are no windows. I worry. What if something bad happens; what if I can't escape, what if we get trapped in here? I have to take Xanax just to get through the session. Twice over the course of classes I throw up in the dimly lit bathroom. Eight weeks in the dark armory, but we come out with a certificate of completion.

Behind my parents' house in Oklahoma is a small pond filled with koi and water plants. There's a stone waterfall and the sound is soothing. Hope loves the pond and every opportunity she has she wades into the water. She splashes around until the fur on her belly is touching the surface. She gets a big drink. This is cute until we notice a smell so foul coming from her that we have to take her to the vet to see what is wrong. I bathe her with medicated shampoo before she goes back to the koi and we realize it is her jaunts into the cool water that are making her smell. Thus begins our endless mission to keep her out of the pond.

We take Hope to a local pet store a few weeks before Christmas to have her picture taken with a man dressed in a Santa suit. I hand her over to him and he wraps his arms around her. She bites his beard and tries to pull it off. When she lets go she shoves her nose up in his face to lick his cheek and knocks his glasses to the floor.

Depression takes away my patience and Hope steals what little of it is left. At Christmas my parents and I put up an artificial tree. Each time Hope bites one of the lower branches and pulls at the tree I want to scream. She is obsessed. The tree twirls around as she scampers around the base with artificial pine in her mouth. I walk over to her, tell her to sit, take my finger and wag it in her face telling her, "No! Bad girl!" She looks at me, then back at the tree. When I turn around I hear the sound of an ornament fall to the floor. We have always left our tree up until after New Year's Day but this year, the morning after Christmas, we take it down.

When Hope is nine months old, we move to North Carolina. As a large puppy, she spends her time getting into mischief. She tears out strips of fiber from the new carpet my parents have just had installed. She digs big holes in the backyard and then leaves muddy paw prints across the hardwood floors. I catch her with her feet on the table so she can reach the food I put on it. I am already stressed out because of the move. Change scares me. I have to find new doctors and therapists. I miss my cousin. I grow frustrated.

A couple months after the move I call my older brother. "I don't think I can keep my dog," I say, swallowing hard to keep from crying.

"Why?"

"She is just annoying everybody. Yesterday she stole our donuts off the dining room table," I say. "There are so many holes in the backyard that Dad is pissed."

"So what are you going to do?"

"I put an ad in the paper to sell her."

"But you love her. She's just a puppy," he says. "She will grow out of it. You just have to hang in there."

"We'll see. Thanks for listening."

"Why don't you come over and hang out with me and Amanda? We could watch a movie or something."

He lives forty-five minutes from my new home and I don't feel up for the drive. "Thanks, but maybe tomorrow."

"All right," he says. "I love you."

The next day I wake up and go downstairs. I open up Hope's crate to let her out and she wiggles with happiness. She puts her front paws on my thighs so I sit down on the floor, exhaling a deep sigh. She rolls onto her back and I rub her warm white belly and begin to cry. How can I get rid of her? I love her. I can't give up on her just because it is difficult, just as I can't give up on life because it is difficult. I have to take care of myself. I have to take care of her.

As Hope gets older she begins to calm down. She is no longer the wild thing she had been as a puppy. Every morning we rise early and go for a walk around the neighborhood. Sometimes I take her into the nearby woods and let her venture into the creek that runs through it. Once or twice a week we take a trip to the park and walk around the lakes. These walks are good for both of us. My doctors tell me that exercise will improve my moods. I notice a change in the way I feel. I start to make plans for the future when up until now it has been a struggle to simply get through the day.

By Hope's second birthday we are living on our own in Wilmington, North Carolina, where I am attending graduate school. Here, she becomes even more important to me. She is my companion and I talk to her in my small apartment like I would talk to a friend. I tell her about the irritating girl in class that I call Laura-who-talks-too-much. I tell her how I feel like I am in over my head. I tell her I have no idea what my professor was talking about today in my fiction workshop when he said "narrative arc."

She sleeps on my bedroom floor every night and the sound of her breathing lulls me to sleep. I wake each morning to her big brown eyes looking at me while her chin rests on the side of the bed. There is a small balcony on my third-floor apartment and we spend hours sitting out on it while I critique classmates' work or write. I put my finger in the whipped cream of my iced mocha and hold it out for her warm tongue to lick off. As I sip my drink Hope watches people coming and going out of the apartment buildings.

Hope makes me feel safe. She weighs more than ninety pounds. When a delivery man comes to the door, I grab her by her collar as she barks. I hold her inside the room as I open the door. The UPS man backs up a few steps and I can see he is afraid as he clutches a small box to his chest. I squeeze out the door and leave her shut in behind me as I sign for the package. I never worry about someone breaking in or attacking me when I take her out for a walk, even late at night. The worries I once had about Ashton, my abusive former boyfriend, coming back to hurt me start to fade.

After I leave graduate school I move in with my boyfriend in Virginia. We have been in a long distance relationship for a year and a half. Hope adores him. Every time she sees him she cries and wags her tail before sitting on his feet so that he will pet her. With the move to Virginia comes the responsibility of another dog, Sammy. He is a sixty-five-pound black and brown dog my boyfriend had rescued a few years before we started dating. We guess that he is part Doberman, but he is still smaller than Hope.

I am usually home during the day while my boyfriend is at work, so Sammy becomes my dog. I feed him, give him treats, take him for rides in the car, let him outside throughout the day. When he has surgery on his leg I apply ointment to the wound religiously. I take him in his cone of shame to the vet every two weeks until his leg heals. He becomes my shadow, following me up and down the steps, sleeping quietly behind me as I type on my computer at my desk. Hope and Sammy play together. He gently bites her mane until she puts her giant paw on his back. They share a water dish and the back seat of my car during rides to the Starbucks drive-thru. And when he also greets me at my bedroom door in the morning I realize he has become one more reason for me to get out of bed.

When you are depressed you need a reason to get up. Hope has often been that reason. I cannot lie in bed all day because the soft, high-pitched whines from behind the bedroom door tell me she needs to go outside. Even if I have no appetite, she hovers around her bowl telling me I must feed her. She cannot do it her-self. She cannot reach the sink or run the water when she needs to refill her water dish.

She needs me.

I believe that Hope, and now Sammy, are an important part

of my wellness. Not only do I love them but they love me back, unconditionally. When I am mad that my life has turned into this storm of clashing moods and medication and doctor visits and therapy and I yell and throw things, they forgive me. Instantly. On days when I wake to depression, a feeling that my best days have come and gone, that it will never be right again, that I am, indeed, a loser, these feelings are jostled around by wagging tails. When I am manic Hope hurries to keep up with me as I try to relieve some of the kinetic energy coursing through my body by going on frantic walks. She waits patiently by the curb as I fall to the grass singing and picking flowering weeds to make daisy chains. To her this is not strange; to her this is happiness.

My dogs give me a reason to live, to pull my shit together and take care of them. They don't ask for much in return for the purpose and companionship they give me, just a little attention, food, water, to be let outside and back in again. It is the most genuine relationship I have. I never have to pretend to be someone I am not. I never have to pretend to feel one way or another. They don't care if I am depressed or manic or anything in between. They love me regardless.

CHAPTER 10

Blog post

The past few days have been...interesting. Saturday night it started. I was filled with energy. It was like I'd drank many, many energy drinks. I spent most of the night on the phone chatting with my sister or my boyfriend. I never once felt sleepy. It is hard to explain—like I could run miles, like I could fly.

I didn't sleep at all that night, never even laid down. After the chattering into the wee morning hours I got on my computer and soon it was light filtering through my window declaring Morning. I still had that energy, that bubbling effervescence inside. I chatted more, felt on the top of the world. Smiling. Laughing. The sky was the limit.

When I've been experiencing days so low it is hard to describe other than black I was given a bright rainbow couple of days. It was a gift, a ray of sunshine, of hope.

I know it can't last, one would become so exhausted, crashing would be inevitable. I am still feeling it a little bit. Sparkly. Blowing glitter from my mouth.

Up Too High

It was early spring 2009, the kind of day that whispers that winter is really over, that the cold I felt would go away, that my twenty-eighth birthday was something to look forward to. I had spent the afternoon with Kimberly, my cousin who was recovering from back surgery. She was my best friend and I spent many of my days with her. As I walked to my car to leave, the sun shone down and I could feel my skin come alive under its caress. I looked up at it, this light shining for me and me alone. I wanted to explode into a hundred pieces and fall upon the grass so green. I wanted to bask in it forever. The energy that I suppressed all day, the feeling that I could run around the block thirty times and not tire, the urge to jump and scream and laugh, was getting harder to control. I got in my car and opened the sunroof so I could bring the sun with me. I plugged in my iPod and turned the volume up on one of my favorite songs. The singer and I had spent a few nights kissing in Austin and I smiled as I remembered his hands on me, his mouth on my mouth. I took the highway home and sang along, remembering how it felt to stand in the crowd, sweating and dancing on a hot Texas night with a whiskey and Coke in my hand, watching him smile and wink at me as he strummed his guitar. As I pulled off onto my exit, I was dying to go faster. I didn't just want speed, I needed it.

The posted limit was forty-five, but the sign wasn't put up for me. It was for people who didn't know how to feel like I felt. I pushed the gas pedal and the car climbed up to seventy. The windows were down and my hair whipped me on the cheeks, stuck to my pink lip gloss. I soared over a hill and pushed the gas pedal harder. Ninety miles an hour. It felt good to obey my mind. I was tired of stifling the urge to move, to let go. One hundred and ten. I could feel the car lift up every time I surged over a hill. I raced past the gravel road leading to my parents' house, slammed on the brakes at the stop sign, then roared ahead. I drove down to Lake Thunderbird and slowed the car as I approached the sharp curve. I pulled into the drive leading to the lake, feeling the seatbelt as it held me tightly, and took a deep breath and brought the car to a jarring stop. I hadn't noticed the way my heart seemed to be beating like the drummer in the song pounding out of the radio. I sat there for a minute. Breathing. Then I aimed the car toward home and willed myself to keep my speed gauge from going above sixty. It felt wrong to go so slowly, like I was running through mud. When I paused at the stop sign, the mud turned to quicksand. I drove on for a few more minutes before easing on the brakes and pulling off onto my road, crunching the gravel beneath the tires for a quarter mile, sending a cloud of dust up behind me.

The revving of the car engine had excited my soul. I had so much to do and needed to do it all right away. I raced through the empty house to my bedroom and tore through the closet. I picked out a silver sequined dress that hugged my hips and showed my thighs. I stripped out of my jeans and T-shirt and pulled the dress over my head. I looked good, so good, but I knew I could look better with a little makeup. I went to the bathroom and began to apply blush in little round pink circles on my cheeks. I reached for my black eyeliner and rimmed my brown-green eyes again and again. Then I took some midnight blue eye shadow and smeared it from my lashes to my eyebrows. I applied layer after layer of mascara, then filled my lips with my brightest red lipstick.

There was so much inside of me that I needed to release. I was brilliant and creative and artistic and beautiful and I needed everyone to know. I grabbed a box of drawing charcoal and rushed outside and through the backyard to the building that housed my mother's photography studio. I flipped on the lights. There was some white backdrop paper hung up on a roll and I pulled on the paper until it spilled on the floor, then ripped off a piece half the size of me and began to draw. I let all my feelings appear there in black and white. I wrote words and then drew hearts and stars over the top until it was just one giant scribble and there was no room left on the page.

My arms and hands were smeared with charcoal when I went back into the house. There was no need to wash the black off. It was a sign that I was an artist. I stepped into the living room and turned on the radio, then cranked the knob until I could feel my body throb with the music. I ran back to my room and grabbed a pair of hot pink high heels and slipped them on. I rushed back to the living room where I found my stage. I stepped onto the coffee table and rose up, writhing to the music. It was here, as I swung my hips and held my hands in the air that some part of my mind returned—perhaps this was mania. I had been manic before, I had seen it in the rearview mirror, but had never recognized it as it was happening. I continued to dance and looked down at my puzzled puppy. She sat a few inches in front of the coffee table and tilted her head to the left as if to ask what the hell I was doing dancing on the furniture. It made me to laugh until I was bent over with black tears streaming down my face.

I danced on that table for twenty minutes. I felt the music. I was the music. And then as suddenly as I had begun, I was finished. What I needed was to climb up high, so I went outside and looked at the towering maple tree in the backyard, twice the height of the house. I kicked my heels off at the base of the trunk and pulled myself up onto the lowest branch. I pulled and pushed and grabbed and lifted until I was higher than the house. Higher than I should have been. I sat there feeling the breeze on my face, inhaling the fresh scent of leaves. I felt the rough bark beneath my smooth thighs. I had never felt so alive. I could do anything.

I sat in the tree, closing my eyes and leaning into the trunk, as my feet dangled below me. After a while, I heard voices. My parents had returned home from dinner. I called out to them, happier than I had been in months.

"Hello!" I said. "I'm up here! Look up in the tree!"

They looked up, first my mother and then my father. What they saw was their daughter, a woman in a sequined dress high up a tree.

"What are you doing up there?" my mother asked, her eyes were wide, her eyebrows raised.

"I climbed the tree!"

"Why did you climb the tree, Elaina?" my dad asked.

"I thought it would be fun! And it was!"

We were all quiet for a minute, them on the ground, me in the tree, though I was the only one who seemed to be happy. Then my mother turned around and opened the door to the house, from which poured the music I had left on. My dad stood there.

"Dad? Could you help me get down?"

I had made my way up without thinking about how to get down. I didn't need to. I was going to live in the tree. Forever.

"Sure, honey," he said and walked over and stood next to my hot pink heels, which looked small from up there. He directed me where to place each foot until he was half catching me as I fell from the tree.

"That was so fun! Thanks for helping me get down," I said as I stood on my tiptoes to give him a hug.

I skipped into the house humming and smiling, skipped right into my room, and sat on the tiny twin bed. My heart was racing and I couldn't keep still. My dad came into the room to check on me.

"What's going on, honey?" he asked.

"I think I'm manic right now. I can't sit still. Here," I said, the words rushed, and took his hand to my throat. "Feel my pulse."

"Your heart is beating really fast, Elaina," he said. "Is there anything I can do for you?"

"I'm good," I said, and smiled. The truth was that I felt great. I didn't want the feeling to ever end. "I think Mom is mad at me."

"She's not mad. She just doesn't know what to do," he said. "I think you scared her."

We sat like that for a while, side by side, on top of blue sheets. The house sounded too quiet without my music. When I finally stopped jiggling my foot as it stuck off the end of the mattress he squeezed my hand.

"You gonna be okay?" he asked.

Twenty minutes had passed since I dropped out of the tree and the pace of my heart had slowed down; the sprint had become a march. I felt uncomfortable, like I'd spent too much time in the sun.

"Yes. It's starting to fade. I'll be fine," I said. "I am just going to sit here for a bit."

He got up from the bed and walked slowly out of my room.

The shaking in my legs had stopped. It was as though all the energy had been sucked out, leaving a deflated body behind. I got up and went to the bathroom and saw what my parents saw—a clown. My makeup was ridiculous and brash. There was a smear of charcoal on my right cheek. My dress was too sparkly for a Wednesday night and there were scrapes on my legs from the bark of the tree.

I have ultra-rapid-cycling bipolar disorder. I swing from mania to depression and back again quickly, sometimes in the span of a single day. My mania has lasted hours; it has lasted weeks. At first it is intoxicating; I am invincible, nothing can touch me. But in the end it becomes unbearable—the sun is too bright, the night is too dark. I am everything and I am nothing. And like a heartbreak it leaves a hole, an ache for what has been. It takes everything you have and leaves you with nothing.

When I am manic, the words can't come fast enough. My tongue gets in the way and my lips are too firm a barrier. I want to talk. I have to talk. The words bubble up inside me until they erupt from my mouth. During an episode of mania in the spring of 2010 that lasted weeks, I met a new group of girlfriends. We went to an Italian restaurant for lunch and as I sat among them I could hardly wait my turn to talk and so I didn't. I interrupted and took control of the conversation, telling them about an intimate fight I had had the night before with my boyfriend. I told them I was ill. I told them that I lived nearby with my parents and about my cousin in Oklahoma. I rattled on about my sister in California and my dog and all the places I had ever lived. For half an hour I held court, allowing only a word or two from the other girls. I could feel the words pouring out but I couldn't stop them. I didn't want to stop them. No one could be as interesting as I was.

When I am manic I can produce endless pages of writing. Essays fly onto my computer screen. Notebooks fill. My blogs grow long. When I read them later, when I am out of my manic state, I am fascinated because I don't remember having written them. It is like reading the prose of someone else. The style is mine. The words are mine. I simply don't remember writing them. Sometimes I reveal too much, just as I do with my mile-a-minute talk. Censorship is erased. There are no safeguards.

Often times when I am manic I think about packing up my car and heading off to somewhere warm. I don't think about where I will end up or how I will get money or how I will pay for a place to live—I just want to disappear. I want to leave without a trace, not so much as a note. During a longer manic episode I decided to leave Virginia and go back to Austin. I got in touch with an old friend and made arrangements to sleep on his couch for an indeterminate amount of time. All I would take with me was a suitcase and my dog. I would get a job down there and a place of my own. I wouldn't need doctors or medicine anymore. I would be just fine. That's the thing about my fantasies; in them I am always well. I no longer swing between mania and depression. The weather will be sunny and I will feel it on my face and that will be enough to cure me.

When the episode subsided, before I packed my bags and filled up the gas tank, reality hit me, as it does each time I come down. Yes, Austin would have been fun for a while, but it would not make me well. I would have bipolar disorder there as I do here or anywhere else I go. I needed my family and my boyfriend and stability. Austin was just another siren's call.

When I'm entering mania I don't sleep. The nights I ventured out on the third-story roof of my parents' house were nights that I barely slept. I just didn't have the need. I was wide awake and raring to go. The day before I hallucinated I stayed up all night watching television and movies waiting for the world to wake up. Often when I am hospitalized there is no rest despite the medication they give me to induce it. I never get tired. I go days on little more than two hours of sleep a night. My energy is boundless. When I do lie still, when I lie in bed and close my eyes, there is an explosion of images people with bipolar disorder call racing thoughts. They come so fast I can't catch one before another takes its place. For me it is like a slide projector in my head. Images flash in my mind for a fraction of a second, one after another. It goes like this: penguin, bicycle, my mom's cinnamon rolls, moon, a hug, sun filtering through leaves, my chipped nail polish, a diamond necklace, a photo of my sister. There is rarely a connection between the thoughts. They come. Relentlessly.

When I overdosed I was manic. I don't know why I took all the Xanax. Something in my mind went away and death came near. I swallowed pills ten at a time—fifty, ninety. I washed them down and waited. I don't know what I was thinking because I can't remember. I wound up in the emergency room and in intensive care. I was hospitalized for days. I tried to kill myself without knowing why. Mania snuck up on me.

My overdose was unplanned. There was a moment when I lost my grip on what was real and opened my mouth. Later came regret and confusion. My friends and family didn't understand. My doctor believed that I had some sort of amnesia when I experienced what he believed to be psychotic breaks caused by my mania. He told me not to feel bad, that it happens. He told me that I don't need to apologize for the things that I have done. He told me I don't have to apologize for having bipolar disorder.

CHAPTER 11

June 27, 2009

Uncle Eric,

Speaking of crazy, I don't like it. Being crazy, I mean. No one ever talks about it, but it's like it's there all the time for me; it doesn't go away. People would just rather not talk about it because it makes them uncomfortable. I think maybe the not talking about it makes me more so. I'm not talking about you, just saying people in general; everyone, really.

I'm hearing things. Apparently, it is common with bipolar people; not all of us have it, but enough that it isn't a concern to the doctors or anything. Boy, was I scared to bring it up, thought I was going more crazy (still feel that way). Out of the corner of my eyes I see things, like I'll think a rat ran by or I think I hear sounds. For example, I just swore the doorbell rang. It didn't. No one is there and I live in the country with my parents. The phantom sights and sounds are considered hallucinations;it isn't the medicine, it's me. The visual ones I'm better able to deal with now, I can dismiss them more easily; the auditory ones can still get me.

I'm tired of thinking crazy thoughts—of being crazy, and I'm tired of living with my parents at twenty-eight and I'm tired of feeling so off I can't drive or trying to get Social Security disability because I can't work. I'm tired of remembering what I used to be able to do and how, because of my medicine, I can remember nothing. Sigh...it just makes me very sad. It's just...broken and I can't fix it. I like to fix things. I am not a complainer, I figure out how to fix it...and I can't. I just have to take it as it comes. It just feels so unfair, like it's taken me miles from who I used to be and I'm not sure who I am anymore. I'm working on that, in thera-

py. Because I'm not Elaina the editor, or Elaina the manager, or Elaina the socialite, or Elaina the "voice of fashion" in Austin, or Elaina who kisses musicians, or Elaina on the radio...I'm just...I don't even know...crazy Elaina? Sorry, that is a lot, but it's what I feel....A lot of the time.

xoxo,

Elaina

Did You See That?

You must die. You must die. You must die, sang the cicadas from the large cottonwood tree, the branches hanging full over the driveway. It was the sound of men with authority, men not to be questioned. They proclaimed it over and over again. You must die! You must die! There were no other commands, no directions on how to do the deed, just that it must be done.

My parents had just pulled out in my dad's pickup, the back heavy with a trailer filled with furniture and boxes. They were off to North Carolina, a two-day drive from Oklahoma and me, standing barefoot by the side of the house. We were moving there, to North Carolina. My parents decided to be nearer my brother and his wife. I had been living with my parents for nine months, since my suicide attempt. It was part of the plan I created in the hospital—stay with my parents until I was well enough to go back out on my own. I wasn't strong enough yet and I couldn't be trusted.

I didn't know if I would have another psychotic break.

"I won't listen to you," I whispered back to the bugs. I padded inside, escaping the sound, the demands. I hadn't been alone five minutes and already I was fighting my mind.

It was getting harder; discerning reality from conjured-up fantasy. It wasn't the shrill vibrations of the cicadas I heard but rather voices telling me what to do, what must be done. And I was trying hard, trying so hard to ignore them. I knew the bugs were just bugs, that bugs couldn't speak and that I was, in fact, crazy. This thought scared me perhaps as much as the thought of killing myself. Somewhere I had crossed the line of sanity, that invisible line between holding it together and losing it.

My parents returned half an hour later; the trailer was packed too unevenly and the weight needed to be redistributed. I was relieved to have them there to ward off the cicadas. I didn't mention the voices. They weren't real and speaking of them would make them so. No, I kept my mouth shut and helped my parents unload and reload the trailer. With my dad close by I heard only the gentle hum of a summer day. The bugs were once again bugs. Sweat trickled down my neck.

After we'd finished playing trailer Tetris, my parents said goodbye once more. This time I did not stand there and see them off. Instead I went inside where it was quiet. I left before the cicadas could sing their terrible song to me.

A few weeks later, after my parents had returned, I was sitting on my bed, blanket askew beneath me. My thoughts were on the essay I was writing on my laptop. Tip, tap, tip, tap. My fingers flew across the keys. I was surprised by someone to my right, standing outside my bedroom door by the washer and dryer. I turned to face her but she was gone.

"Hello?" I said. "Mom, is that you?"

Silence.

"Mom?" I walked into the kitchen and through the dining room. I found my mom at the other end of the house, sitting at her own computer. "Were you just over by my room?"

"No, I've been right here checking my email," she said.

I knew I had seen someone, but my mom and I were the only ones home. If it wasn't her standing outside my room who had it been? This wasn't the first time I questioned what I saw. I didn't want to admit to myself that what I believed was there was all in my head, my messed-up head. But I was tracking down ghosts now. Always my calls went unanswered; always the person disappeared before I could face them.

Though people often appeared out of nowhere, the bugs dominated. I stood in the bathroom when a cockroach crawled out from beneath the closet door. I raised my foot and slammed it down on the pale pink tiled floor. There was no satisfying crunch beneath my blue flip-flop, just rubber on tile. I raised my foot. Nothing. I scanned the floor in search of the roach. There was no way such a big bug could disappear that quickly. I checked my flip flop again. Nothing.

The Tuesday after I had tried to squash the roach, I was sitting in the dining room eating my breakfast. Along the wall crawled a brazen bug, taunting me.

Here I am. I am real. You know I am.

But I didn't. I couldn't. I rolled up a magazine and swung at the dark spot on the wall. The spot disappeared and left me alone and confounded.

Sitting in the waiting room of the psychiatric clinic, I began to swat at the swarm of flies, at least five of them, buzzing so near I could hear them. I swatted at them trying to keep them out of my face.

I tried to sit still but they kept buzzing around my head. The middle-aged woman in the ill-fitting jeans and the "Florida" T-shirt sitting across from me was staring. The blond man who had been sitting next to me returned from the bathroom and chose a bank of seats on the other side of the room. I got up and walked to the water fountain. The flies didn't follow me. When I came back to my seat they were gone. I discreetly tried to look around the room to find out where they had come from and where they had gone, but I couldn't see them anymore. I couldn't hear them. They had disappeared. I was left with nothing but questions: why, when I went after these bugs, did they disappear? Why didn't I crush anything? Why did no one else ever see them?

Sometimes the moving target was bigger. In my periphery I'd see it scamper across the floor. Four legs and a tail. Brown. Gray. Small and furry. I've always abhorred rodents. My years in New York City cemented these feelings. Dirty little creatures.

I'd scream in my Brooklyn apartment when a mouse ran across the hardwood floor in the kitchen. My roommates laughed it off. It was just a mouse, they'd say, but to me it was a predator out to get me. My feet flew up onto the couch as I tucked them safely beneath me, or my knees were hugged to my chest in fear.

Once in my apartment on the Upper West Side I'd reached for a snack and noticed my crackers were stale. The corner of the bag was nibbled through. Disgusted, I spit the food into my hand and from then on kept all food in my tiny refrigerator. Then there were the subway stations. While waiting for the trains I would watch the rats as they scurried around the tracks looking for food. Dirty as the filth they squandered in, dark as night. It made me nervous. I worried about them touching me, bringing that decay to my skin, their mouths on my flesh.

So, when these years later I began to see these defiled tiny creatures out of the corner of my eye, I was scared. I regarded them with the same attitude. But when I turned my head to see them, they were gone. They were too quick. Each and every time they disappeared before I could focus on them.

I stood in the kitchen of my parents' house on my tiptoes and grabbed a plastic cup from the top shelf of the cabinet. As I brought it down I saw a mouse run along the floorboard. Screaming I dropped the cup on the counter and it bounced to the floor. The mouse had disappeared beneath the cabinet where we kept the pots and pans. My mother came rushing into the room.

"What's wrong?" she asked.

"There was a mouse!" I exclaimed.

"A mouse?" she asked.

"Yes! It just ran along there and disappeared in that cabinet," I told her pointing to the floor. She walked over and opened the cabinet. I waited for it to run out at me, to run somewhere, but there was no mouse.

"See," she said, "there's nothing there."

She looked at me for what felt like a long time. This was not the first time I had seen a mouse. There had been the one in the bathroom and the one in the garage. There had been a few sightings outside on the porch. To appease me my parents set out mouse traps, though I was the only one seeing these rodents and I was seeing them everywhere. My mom was beginning to understand that what I thought I saw and what I actually saw were two different things. I wondered for a moment if she thought I was crazy; if she knew I was.

During these months of seeing bugs and mice and shadows, I also heard things, phantom noises. It wasn't just bugs talking to me. The doorbell would ring or someone would say my name. But when I opened the door no one was there. When I called back no one answered. I spent a lot of time asking, "Did you hear that?" but no one ever did. It was just me and my mind and its tricks.

The only person I felt comfortable talking to was my psychiatrist. It was too scary to tell anyone else. What if they knew I was crazy? Would they send me away? Would I have to go back to the psych ward again? It had only been months that I had been out. I sat in my doctor's office and softly spoke.

"I've been seeing things," I said, "things that aren't really there."

"Like what?" he asked, looking up from his prescription pad.

"Well, there are a couple of things...There are a lot of bugs and there are mice. I keep seeing people, too. It is always in the periphery of my vision and when I turn to them they disappear," I said. "...And I'm hearing things, too."

I waited for him to show concern or shock or disgust. I didn't know what to do but sit there with my hands kneading my thighs.

"This is normal. Hallucinations come and go with bipolar patients," he said.

I felt my caught breath release from my chest. My heart slowed.

"Really?"

"Yes. Some people get them and some people don't. You may have them a lot or rarely. We'll have to wait and see."

I watched him in silence as he finished writing the prescriptions. I wasn't sure what to make of this new information. Part of me was relieved that I wasn't going crazy, that this was somewhat normal and to be expected, but part of me was scared. Would I always see and hear things? Was this just a precursor to what was in store?

Hallucinations are usually associated with schizophrenia, but they are also common to people with bipolar disorder. Hallucinations involve hearing, seeing, feeling, smelling, and even tasting things that are not real. But I didn't know this. I was given no instruction book on how to deal with this illness. No one told me what to expect. No one sat me down and said, "Elaina, you may see things or hear things. Hell, you could feel or taste things that aren't real! This is completely normal for someone like you. Don't be scared. This is just another symptom, not a sign of you losing your mind."

When I wrote the email to my uncle it was the first time I told someone other than my psychiatrist about my hallucinations. I chose to confide in my Uncle Eric because I trusted him. He told me his secrets and I told him mine. He is ten years older than me—old enough to be wiser, but young enough to be understanding. He called me "Peanut." He made me feel safe. With him I opened up and became vulnerable. It didn't necessarily feel good to get it out, to say the things I felt every day, but I needed solace. I needed someone to tell me that everything was going to be okay. I wanted, more than anything, for someone to take it all away. I didn't want to hear things or see things that weren't real. I didn't want to be bipolar, not then, not before, not after. I wrote the email to my uncle in hopes of salvation, a salvation that never came.

My psychiatrist and I played around with different medications to treat my bipolar disorder and my hallucinations lessened. Eventually they seemed to vanish. It would be years before I experienced them again. The next time would be during a manic episode. It would be brief and bearable. It made the psychiatrist's statement true—they would come and go.

The important thing to remember was that they would go.

CHAPTER 12

Blog post

I was sitting in my boyfriend's black Dodge Ram 1500 in the middle of a thunderstorm. We were stuck in traffic due to a gas line break on the cross street we were approaching. Add to that rush hour traffic being diverted and you have a recipe for idling. There was something playing on the radio and he sang along with it. I love to hear him sing. I could curl up on his lap like a cat and listen for hours. He was holding my hand in his. His hand is strong and masculine and dwarfs my own. There was this feeling in my chest—a tightness, a bursting. As I looked at him I thought, I don't know how I could ever love you any more than I do right this minute. And so I said it, because I meant it. He just smiled and told me he loved me and kissed my pink-polished fingers. The truth is that there isn't a word big enough for my feelings for my boyfriend. Love is only four letters; I feel an entire language.

I have been in love before, more than once. I am lucky. But I have never been in a relationship that has lasted this long. I have never lived with a boyfriend before him. I have never been this comfortable in my own skin. I know that he loves me, without a doubt, one hundred percent.

And that's the thing about love, there is always room for more. Even when I think there is no way I could love him more, I will wake up tomorrow and feel him wrapped around me and know that somehow there is more love in my heart.

Him

I am never alone with my bipolar disorder. Even when I am sitting on the bathroom floor slitting my wrist, I am not alone.

Even in the dark on the roof, I am not alone. I am swirling around in the minds of those who love me, always in their thoughts and prayers. My life permeates theirs. It demands attention: The phone calls when I've overdosed, the visits to the hospital, my exploding anger, the worry about what's coming next. I have alienated family members, lost friends. But along the way I have found someone to hold my hand. He stands close by as my moods slam one into another. He is, just maybe, the most patient man on the planet.

I met Jeremy in high school, a decade before the madness came. He was a friend who dated one of my friends. I remember him as shy and quiet. After high school he joined the Navy and made it a career. He went on to marry that high school friend and have three kids with her. Then, after ten years, things with his wife crumbled. I was just beginning to recover from my suicide attempt. Things weren't good but they were looking up. A mutual friend of ours suggested I get in touch with him; that he was having a hard time, too, and maybe we could help each other.

I contacted him through MySpace and we began to chat.

"Hey, old friend," I typed. "Sounds like you could use a cheer-leader, and it just so happens that I used to be one."

"Oh, I remember!" he said. "Yeah, things have been pretty shitty, but I am talking to you so maybe it isn't so bad."

"I was thinking I could use a little sunshine. What do you think about an Oklahoma girl coming out to the beach?"

"It is a popular spot," he said. "That would be cool."

I smiled at my computer screen.

"What would a guy say to ask a cheerleader out?"

"You just ask her."

"Wanna go out?"

I was living with my parents in Oklahoma and Jeremy was stationed in Virginia Beach, so there were a lot of emails and fe-verish typing as we chatted online. Then, one day, as I was stand-ing outside of the clinic following a bipolar disorder support group meeting, I felt brave and used the number he had given me. The phone rang twice before he picked up. I don't remember what we said, but what I remember about that short conversa-tion as I stood at the curb waiting for my mother to pick me up was his voice. It was warm and gentle and I didn't want it to ever stop talking to me.

After that we talked a lot, often late into the night. Sometimes we would talk during the day and I would sit beneath the maple tree in the backyard, trying to get a cell phone signal out there in the country at my parents' home. It was nice that way, the way things began. We got to know each other without anything physical to mess it up. There was no pressure, just the enjoyment of the other's voice on the line.

We talked about our dreams and desires, the little things and the big. Jeremy read all my blog posts on MySpace. It allowed him to get inside my head, he said, to wander through my words. Later he would tell me that he fell in love with me through my writing. It was one of the things he loved best.

"Don't be mad at me, but I did something," he said.

"What did you do?" I asked.

"I did something for you that you really wanted but I don't know if you will be mad at me or not."

"You're scaring me," I said. "What are you talking about?"

"Well, you know how you wanted a blog website? I made you one."

"What?"

"Yeah. I made you one. Go to elainaj.com. You said you really wanted one and it was something I could do for you so I did it," he said. "Are you mad?"

I went to the site and opened it up and there, staring back at me, were my eyes.

"I'm not mad, not at all." I said. "I can't believe you did this."

"I was so afraid you would be mad," he said. "I didn't ask you before doing it."

Tears filled my eyes. This was an act of kindness and I needed kindness. I needed someone who did more than listen to me; I needed someone who would help. The site became somewhere I could go and talk without being interrupted. I could talk about my illness and what it felt like to be sick. I could talk about what it meant to be well. I fell in love with Jeremy.

When I met him again in person, for the first time in ten years, it was at my brother's house in North Carolina. We had been talking for a couple of months but still hadn't seen each other. I waited on the porch in a white wooden rocker. I heard his truck before I saw it. He pulled into the driveway and I stood up, heart pounding. I walked over as he hopped out of his Dodge Ram pickup and came around the front. He wore a black T-shirt, jeans, and a blue walking boot that went up to his knee, to support the ankle he broke in a car crash a month prior. He was a few inches taller than me—not tall, but tall enough. He was slim, as my boyfriends all tended to be. His hair was buzzed short, a military cut, and I noticed his eyes were the color of the Caribbean Sea. When he smiled I realized I had been holding my breath.

Jeremy tentatively stepped towards me, leading with his good ankle, and put his arms around me. When we pulled apart we were both smiling. He had driven to North Carolina to spend the weekend with my family and help me paint my new room in my parents' new home. I was no longer living halfway across the country. Now we were just four hours apart.

It is hard to remember a time when I didn't trust him, but in the beginning, I guess I didn't. I hadn't had a serious boyfriend since Ashton. Ashton had told me he loved me and yet tried to push me out of a speeding car. Although I had dated a few nice guys since Ashton, I wondered, would this new boyfriend hurt me too? I gave him pieces of my heart, a little at a time, until eventually he held it all. He tells me that he would never hurt me and I am sad that he even has to say that, that it had ever been any other way.

It was a few months into our relationship when I told Jeremy I was bipolar. I had hinted about being sick but not come right out and stated what exactly was wrong with me. He didn't ask and I didn't say and we carried on like that for a while. The word bipolar was on the tip of my tongue but I couldn't say it. I was afraid he would leave and so many had gone away already. But as I grew more comfortable in our relationship I grew more confident that he just might stay.

"I'm bipolar," I said softly into my phone late one night, him on the other end.

"Okay," he said. "What can I do?"

He didn't run, he didn't make me feel ashamed or weak; he did what he always did, he showed compassion. He was relieved because he had thought I was perhaps dying, and this was not death, this was a mental illness. He didn't know that up to a third of all of those who suffer from bipolar disorder commit suicide, that bipolar disorder is the second-most leading cause of suicide in women.

I told him about my suicide attempt, which felt fresh even then, less than a year later. He was relieved because I had failed, but was also shocked because he had no idea what I had been through, what I was still going through. Most of all, he was sad.

I love to hold his hand—in the car, on long walks, watching a movie. Skin to skin. Jeremy's hand is bigger than mine and tough and manly. It is our way of saying you are mine and I am yours. It gives me a sense of security that I am not alone, that I am cared about and protected.

I shared with him early about my obsessive compulsive disorder. I was afraid it would change things. That this was one more thing that might push him away when all I wanted to do was pull him close. But his response to my OCD was understanding. In the beginning, and oftentimes today, my OCD gets the better of me. I count and I line things up and I wash my hands over and over again. But he holds my menus for me and opens my doors so I don't have to touch them. He lets me perform my ritual of washing out cups and doesn't say a word. He knows not to tease me, that I can't stop once I start. It has become as much a part of our relationship as kissing.

With him I am beautiful and sexy, even without makeup, first thing in the morning. And that is where I love him most—in the bedcovers. When he has his arm wrapped around me and his nose nuzzled in my neck. I can feel his breath on my skin and I am safe.

He tells me that the hardest part of my illness is seeing me depressed. He can see it when it comes. He can hear it in the way that I talk. Everything takes an effort I don't have. It is all I can do to lift my toothbrush to my mouth. I don't want to get out of bed and one bad day turns into another and another until there is a long succession of bad days and I feel like they will go on forever. Everyone has bad days, he says, but for me it takes a lot longer than one day to feel better.

His biggest fear is that I will end my life when he is not there. Jeremy has seen me in the throes of depression, when things are so dark I cannot see the light. He has listened to the sadness in my voice. He has seen me overdose; take enough pills to stop my breathing. He worries that one day he will come home and find that I have succeeded.

Our relationship is unfair. He shouldn't have to deal with the volatile clash of my moods. He shouldn't have to sit next to the bath as I cry and my mascara runs and I become a snotty mess. He shouldn't have to stop the bleeding or call my mother. It isn't fair and I tell him often. But he tells me he loves me, all of me, even the sick parts and the sad parts.

I have been hospitalized twice in our relationship and I have never allowed him to visit me. I don't want him to see me like that—messy hair, hospital slippers, sedated speech, and that lost look in my eyes. I want him to think of me in my favorite black dress and lipstick. I want him to think of the good times. He calls me and we talk for the five or ten minutes I am allowed on a phone in the hallway as a schizophrenic man loiters next to me and a sad girl sits on the floor waiting for someone to call her. He finds relief in the fact that I am safe, that there is an entire staff to watch me. He believes that maybe they can fix what is wrong. But most of all, when I am locked away from the world, he misses me. He wants to fall asleep with me in his arms. He wants to tuck me in when he leaves for work in the morning. He wants a kiss when he gets home. When I am gone there is a hole.

He came as a package deal—three kids, ages five, seven, and nine. I wasn't used to kids and suddenly I had a ready-made family. In the beginning, when our relationship was long distance, I rarely saw the children. I visited when they were not with him or he would come see me on weekends he didn't have them. After a year and a half together I moved in and all that changed. I saw them every other weekend and sometimes longer at Christmas break and in the summer. I grew accustomed to them and created a life that included them. Strawberry picking on my birthday. Pumpkin carving for Halloween. Making muffins on Saturday mornings with his oldest daughter. And every time I would see my boyfriend kiss one of his children or pick up the littlest one and carry him to bed, I would fall a little more in love.

He doesn't see my illness through the same eyes. I focus on the what ifs—what if I go back to the hospital, what if I become manic again, what if I become so depressed I cannot move, what if I try to take my life again? He says I focus too much on the negative aspects of my illness and don't give enough credit to the good times. He doesn't anticipate my next hospitalization. He sees it as a possibility, not a certainty. He chooses not to plan for it because no one knows when it will happen again. It's a bridge to cross when we get there. He knows we can deal with it because we already have.

My unpredictable moods affect our relationship. I have nearly called it quits a dozen times. It isn't him, it is me. When I am depressed I can only feel an ache so big I think I might die from it. And how can I have a relationship when I can hardly breathe? How can I love someone else when I can't love myself?

He says he's Superman because he saves me. Every day. He makes me happy and in this happiness I find hope. I can imagine that things will get better and that I am, in fact, good enough. He says it is hard to get depressed when you are already happy and I think there is some truth in that. It's harder to reach the ground when you are up so high.

No one should hurt his baby. That is what he says to me. He can't understand why I cut my wrist. He knows that there comes a desire in me so strong that I cannot extinguish it. Every time I have cut I have been "out of it," he says. It's not the real me, it is the bipolar me. He can't sympathize and he fucking hates it. But when I am manic I don't think about consequences or how I affect anyone else. There is only me. I leave no room for him.

He can see my depression but not my climb into mania. He only knows it once I am there. I climb onto roofs and stay up all night. I forget everything even as it is happening. Sometimes I think all is wonderful and I am wonderful and I want to share my brilliance with the world. Other times it leads to a mixed episode in which the power of my mania gives me the energy to act on my depressed feelings. This is when it is the most dangerous. He watches me closely when I am flying. He knows I will crash.

With him I am not crazy, never crazy, despite sometimes acting the opposite. Jeremy lets me be me and I can trust him with all that I am. I can tell him I am throwing up again. I can tell him I want to cut. He listens and he holds me in the dark, tells me it will be okay, saves me again.

He says I am defiant when I am manic. He says if he tells

me not to do something, then I will do it more fervently. He says I have three personalities. Manic. Depressed. And me. He says when I am manic I can be super happy, but also defiant. When I am depressed there is no reasoning with me. And when I am me, well, when I am me he loves me best.

Jeremy's love is unconditional. He soothes me. I want to curl up on his lap and stay there forever. His love is so great that he tells me if it were possible, he would take my place. He would fight my battles for me and stare into the abyss. I wonder if I could love him in the way that he loves me if our roles were reversed. Could I care for someone who is sometimes so sick? Do I possess the hope and the compassion and the patience?

We face this together; side by side. He cannot save me but he can hold my hand, keep me from falling, keep me from flying away.

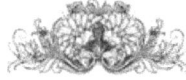

CHAPTER 13

Blog post

Blue. Electric. It threads through my skin, holding it together, putting my pieces back together. There are tiny knots as though a fairy climbed upon my skin and sewed it while I slept in the hospital bed.

For the last five days I have been confined to a fortress of mercy. Cream colored walls. Cold tiled floors. Beeping. The rattling of pills, so many pills. Questions. "How are you feeling today, on a scale of 1–10?" "How would you rate your pain?" Leave me alone. I'm sick. I'm tired. I'm sick and tired of you.

Eyes shut. IVs. I need rest.

Beneath the surface of the jagged puzzle pieces jammed together and wrapped in the pretty electric blue bow lies illness. Wrongs I cannot make right. Deals that cannot be unmade. They were created when I was and so we live together. They sleep silently below the surface until days like these, until days like the last five.

As anyone with an ailment not visible to the eye will tell you, it is impossible to describe to others what it feels like on the inside. I imagine it has the effect of describing color to a blind man. So we swallow it all down—the razorblades and bile and loneliness— and tire. The educated, the afflicted and the doctors will understand and that must be enough for us.

Sleeping was futile. There was always a light on, always a noise in the hall, always discomfort when I moved. Nurses demanded vital checks even when the sun had escaped them. They roused me to take this pill, now take that. Up one side of the bed and round to the other. TV for days and none of it good, save a movie or two.

This is my second hospitalization in a little over a year and not likely to be my last...and it's hard. Hard to be sick and hard to be treated as such. And some days, some days things feel just fine and I smile and it's actually authentic and even if life isn't good I can imagine how it might be.

Again

The paper towel bled crimson beneath my fingers. I hadn't meant to cut so deep. I only meant to cut a little bit to silence the voices in my head, the voices insisting that I cut my wrist. Again and again they spoke until it was only natural to follow their direction. I had used a knife this time instead of the X-Acto blade. It wasn't easy to judge the depth of the cut, metal to flesh.

I heard my parents return from the store in the house below me and called out. I didn't dare move. I sat still, my hold tight around my wrist, and waited. My parents were quick up the stairs. They could tell by the pleading in my voice there was trouble. It was the same trouble that hid behind my eyes, always there, waiting. It was first my dad, his eyes wide as he took me in. My mom followed moments after.

"What have you done?" she asked, and I didn't have an answer. I had, for a moment, lost it and when I came to there was a two-inch gash in my left wrist.

"Do you want to go to the hospital?" my mom asked. I needed stitches to sew my flesh back together, but going to the hospital meant I would have to stay. They would think I was trying to kill myself again. But going to the hospital didn't sound too bad. I needed a break from my life. It had become heavy, a burden. Happiness eluded me. Dark thoughts made my head murky.

I followed my mom to my bedroom, my grip still tight. I directed her to pack my sweatshirts and the sweatpants bought during my last hospitalization a little over a year prior. I told her where to find my hospital socks and my underwear. In our hurry we grabbed bottles and tubes from the bathroom. I left my razor and my hair dryer, things they don't allow you the luxury of having in a psych ward. The pink Bic could be used to cut my wrists and the hairdryer cord could be used to strangle myself. If I took them they would be held for me at the nurses' station until my release. I left them behind with my dog and my bed and my life.

The hospital was close. I remembered what peace that brought me when we moved into the neighborhood. I felt safe, wrapped up in the fact that I wouldn't need an ambulance. I could be driven there in a matter of minutes. I was counting on needing the hospital from the moment we moved in. That's the thing with bipolar disorder; you know that one day it will catch up with you. You don't know when or how, but you know it will. You never take for granted a day when your mood isn't flying from one extreme to the other. You never get too comfortable.

We arrived at the hospital on the middle of that cold January day. We walked in and went up to the nurses' station.

"My daughter's cut her wrist," my mom told the nurse. Immediately I was taken back to a hospital bed. I lay down and watched as a young nurse with curly brown hair inserted an IV. My dad left us then. He wasn't one for hospitals and he once again found himself wondering how this had happened. What was wrong with his little girl that made her hurt herself? What made her flirt with death so carelessly? Next to my hospital bed sat my mother. A doctor came to me.

"What did you do?" he asked me.

"I cut my wrist," I told him.

"What did you use?"

"I used a knife from the kitchen."

"You'll need a tetanus shot then but first let's get this cut taken care of," he told me, a bit gentler than before.

He shot something into the flesh on either side of the cut, numbing it so I wouldn't feel the needle he stuck into my wrist. I watched him in a state of calm. It all seemed very matter-of-fact. I had cut myself and now had to be sewn back together. It didn't hurt. He was quick and efficient, creating five small stitches. He put a gauze pad on the wound and then wrapped it up in a flesh-colored bandage. Around and around my wrist it went.

It seemed a lot of fuss for something so small. I didn't need all this—the IV, the hospital bed, the tetanus shot. I simply needed to be sewn up and I would have been on my way. But wrist cutting is not taken lightly by hospital staff. I lay on the bed for an hour before a hospital psychologist found me. He stood next to my mom, looking haggard and older than his thirty-some years.

"I'm Dr. Howard, a hospital psychologist. I'm here because we are alarmed that you have cut yourself. Why did you cut yourself?" he asked me.

"I couldn't get the thought out of my head. I cut myself sometimes when the urge won't go away. I didn't mean to cut myself so deeply."

"Well, the problem is that you can't cut your wrists regardless of how deep you meant to cut. We view this as a suicide attempt and unfortunately we'll have to keep you here," he explained.

"Okay," I said. "I figured I'd have to. I brought my stuff."

He wrote on his clipboard something about me. They all had their opinions—suicidal, psychotic, manic, depressed. But in the end it didn't matter what term you slapped on it, to me it meant crazy.

Time and again I would ask the nurse to unhook my IV so I could stumble down the emergency room to the bathroom. It was a small, private bathroom and I was thankful for the privacy. As I moved to wash my hands my hospital gown fell open. I was having trouble keeping the fabric I was swimming in over my breasts. I wrapped myself up and crossed my arms below my bust and made my way back. My mom waited patiently by my bed, my temporary tether to reality. Her gray hair was pulled back in a long ponytail and behind her glasses her green eyes flashed concern when she looked up at me. After a few hours a nurse with kind eyes stopped to ask me if I was hungry. I hadn't eaten since breakfast and so she brought me a tray. A sandwich, an apple, and green jello. I picked the bread off the sandwich and ate it hungrily. My vegetarian appetite didn't allow for meat. I tried to share what little I had with my mother but she was in no mood for food. To her I was just a little girl lying in a hospital bed. My age fell away, leaving behind the eyes, the mouth she had always known. This wasn't the first time I was hospitalized and she knew it wouldn't be the last.

I stayed a few hours in the emergency room. Then I was taken upstairs to the psych ward. I had to tell my mother goodbye. That was always the hardest part, saying goodbye. When you were admitted. When they visited. There was always a goodbye. And when they turned to leave you were left alone with the madness.

I was shown to a private room. It was bare bones—bed, chest of drawers, desk and chair. There was a bathroom in the room and on the door was a Hawaiian scene, a sunset, or maybe it was a sunrise, with palm fronds arguing for space. Inside was a toilet and a sink. I was thankful for the privacy this allowed me. Privacy is hard to come by in psych wards. The camera in the corner of my room proved it. But I was given this little piece of paradise and didn't have to share my island with anyone.

"I'm from Queens," he said.

"I lived in New York on and off for two and a half years," I said. I had. Ages ago, before I was conversing with a schizophrenic in the psych ward, I had lived in Brooklyn and Manhattan. I had worked in the fashion industry. My life was a whirlwind of fashion shows and keeping track of dresses for magazine photo shoots. It had been exhilarating at first. I was just a girl from Oklahoma when I arrived, but a young lady from New York when I left. But back then I wasn't bipolar, at least not noticeably so. I was simply depressed on and off. I had yet to learn about manic episodes, yet to experience them. I hadn't yet hallucinated or cut my wrist. I hadn't overdosed or nearly died. I had simply lived the life of a girl in the big city.

"Really?" he asked. "What part?"

"Well, I lived in Carroll Gardens in Brooklyn for a year. And in the ghetto of Brooklyn for a summer. And then in Manhattan. Times Square for a summer and then the Upper West side for about a year."

"Cool. What are you doing in North Carolina?" he asked.

"I live with my parents and they moved out here this past summer."

"Cool. Why are you in here?"

He was dark skinned, like he might have been from Puerto

Rico instead of Queens. His hair was wavy and black and he had deep brown eyes. I could feel myself opening up to this stranger. I could see myself as though out of my body having a conversation with someone I deemed sane in all this craziness.

"I cut my wrist," I said and held up my wrapped up wrist.

"Why?" he asked.

"I don't know...I wasn't trying to kill myself," I added. "What about you? You seem sane enough."

"Don't let me fool you," he winked at me. "I'm schizophrenic. I had an episode, let's leave it at that. How long you in for?"

"I don't know yet. I have to see the doctor tomorrow. You?"

"Friday. Fourteen-day hold."

It was Sunday, which meant he had been on the inside for nine days. It was only my second day in and I could hardly imagine what thirteen more might do to me.

"I'm Jay," he said.

"Elaina. Nice to meet you."

A large nurse came in. She wore faded blue scrubs and the hem of her right pant leg was frayed. She told us that group was starting in a few minutes and to move to the dining room. Jay and I got up slowly and walked to the large room filled with six tables surrounded by blue plastic chairs. We sat down at the same table and listened to a presentation on the importance of personal hygiene.

The following morning, freshly showered, I met with the psychiatrist. I was nervous. I always was when I met a new doctor. I knew that I would have to talk about all the things that were wrong with me. It was embarrassing and unpleasant and I preferred not to do it. I had a problem admitting I was sick even when I was hospitalized.

He was a big man in his late fifties, with sparse gray hair. He sat behind an oak desk with a nameplate that read Phillip White, M.D. I noticed the way his neck swelled beneath his tie and the sweat on his upper lip. In front of him was a folder of papers— my file. He looked up only when I entered the room and then stared at the writing in front of him. He asked me a few questions, the same ones I was always asked. Had I been hospitalized before? Was I seeing a psychiatrist? Had I been diagnosed? Was

I on any medication? Was it helping? Why was I in the hospital again? How was I feeling about the future? I gave him my litany of answers. I explained my life in a few short breaths. I told him I was feeling better, that I lived with my parents and that I would be seeing my psychiatrist once I was out. I told him what I needed to tell him to be released. It wasn't a lie, just a tailored truth. Finally, he looked up and met my gaze.

"I'd like to keep you for a while longer," he said. "Let's tentatively say you can go home Friday."

"Really? That long?" I said.

"Yes," he said and began shuffling the papers on his desk. "I think that is best."

I nodded. "Okay." I got up and walked out of his office and back to my room and sat down on the plastic mattress of my bed. It was longer than the last time. My doctor had warned me that each time I was hospitalized it would be for a longer stay than the previous trip. I looked up at the sunset on the door and felt my eyes burn as tears slid down my face.

There were two rooms for the patients to gather—the dining room and the great room. In the great room was a television that was on from morning until night. The nurses kept the remote; the decision of what to watch was taken from us. The chairs were arranged in several rows facing the television with a few chairs surrounding them. There were a couple of end tables along the walls, between the chairs, and on them were stacked old Reader's Digest books. There were a few coloring books and baskets of crayons. There was no occupational therapy at this hospital, no real therapy at all. We attended a group or two a day where the nurses presented information—how to look for a job, the importance of staying on your medication. Meals broke up the day. Our food came on plastic trays. Again there were no caffeinated beverages or metal utensils. We didn't have a choice of meals; you ate what you were given or you didn't eat at all.

The highlight of the day came at six o'clock in the evening; that was visiting hour. Everyday my mother came. She never came empty handed. She brought me food—a sandwich to replace my poor dinner; cookies, chips. She brought me a book to read. She never showed fear or disappointment, only love. She would tell me about her day and I would tell her about the other patients, about the fights and the breakdowns and the outbursts. Two guests were allowed for each patient, so most days my dad came with her, but on Tuesday evening my brother came. He had never been to see me in the hospital; he wasn't in California the first time. All six-foot-one inches of him slouched on the plastic chair. I watched him as his hazel eyes darted around the room uneasily. His long fingers fidgeted with the cargo pocket on his thigh.

"How you feeling?" he asked, looking up at me.

"Oh, I'm fine. Ready to get out of here." I wanted to make him feel better. I didn't like the sadness I saw around his mouth, didn't like that I was the cause of it.

"Maybe next weekend you could come over for dinner or something," he said.

"Yeah, that would be nice."

When he stood to leave he wrapped me in his arms and hugged me. I was so much smaller than he was and for a moment I felt safe. I wanted to follow him out the doors that locked behind him when he walked away with my mother. I stood there staring at the doors long after they had left.

One evening during visiting hour my mother stared at one of the patients.

"He just put some crayons in his pockets!"

"Who?" I asked and turned to look. "Oh, that's Fred. He's schizophrenic. He flies off the handle all the time, sometimes at no one in particular. I've caught him taking pieces of the puzzles too. I guess he's a klepto."

"You meet some of the most interesting people in here, Elaina," she said, and winked at me.

The following day I realized my book was missing. I searched my room and then went ambling around the great room and dining room. Finally, I walked up to Fred, who was consumed with a picture of a unicorn he was coloring.

"Fred, have you seen my book?"

"Nope," he said, without looking up.

"Are you sure?" I asked. I wondered if he had taken it back to his room with the rest of his stash.

"Who are you?! Why don't you leave me alone?! I hate you! I hate you! I hate you!" His hands went to his head and he started to hit himself. He emitted a noise somewhere between a grunt and a scream and I took a few steps backward into the last row of chairs. The nurses rushed in and tried to calm him down. They asked me what had happened and I told them.

"I hate you! I'll kill you! I will! I will kill you!" he yelled fixing his eyes on me.

They led him from the room as he continued to scream at me, foul language filling the air. I felt the eyes of everyone on me like a heavy coat. My heart beat loudly in my ears. I turned around and walked out of the great room and down the long hallway to my own room. I sat on my bed and pulled my knees to my chest, scared. I stayed away from Fred after that. I avoided eye contact and was sure to sit as far from him as I could. He was delusional and dangerous and I was just trying to survive.

One evening as my mother and father sat with me in the dining room discussing our days, my eyes landed on a new patient. He was in his late sixties, sitting in a corner of the room, and biting off the bandages on his arms. I watched as he bit down on the latex and pulled with his crooked teeth. His head jerked as he pulled and then, one by one, spit them out.

"Just a minute, Mom." I got up and walked out to the nurses' station.

"Hi. There is a patient who is pulling off his bandages in the dining room," I said to José, the short male nurse.

"Thanks," he said and got up and followed me back.

By the time we entered the room his IV was out and the bandages were at his feet. The nurse walked over to him and said something quietly. The older man got up and followed the nurse out of the room. Ten minutes later I saw him walking down the hallway to his room, with a larger bandage on his arm, but this time the IV was missing.

The days passed slowly. I would stare at the television for hours. Every once in a while a call would come in for me. My boyfriend called and asked to come and visit me but I told him no. I didn't want him to see me in there. I wanted to hide the crazy. I read my book until it went missing. I attempted to do a jigsaw puzzle but was annoyed to find half of the pieces gone. Some patients played cards with incomplete decks. Some spent their time huddled near the phone, waiting for calls that never came.

It was a floor filled with disappointment.

There was a perpetual tension in the air of something about to happen—a fight, a cry, an explosion. Someone would sit in the corner, moving his mouth, inaudible, tears streaming down his face. I learned to leave people alone, that I could not fix what was broken. When you bring the angry and the delusional together a spark is bound to be created. A wrong glance, a loud word, and someone would burn with fire. The nurses were not mediators, but rather wardens. They kept people apart, sent them to their rooms, administered drugs to sedate them. I learned to keep to myself, rarely speaking. I chose just a couple people I felt were safe enough, sane enough, to talk to. We were all fighting our own illnesses, diagnosed but uncured.

When I was locked away I realized the value of my freedom. I remembered what it felt like to take a walk outside and feel the sun on my face. I craved a hot cup of coffee with cream. I missed taking a long, hot shower. I worried that my dog didn't understand where I'd gone. I wanted to have phone conversations that lasted longer than five minutes. I missed my bed and soft sheets. I needed my hairdryer. I realized all I took for granted when I was outside hospital walls. It was the little things that got to me, that built up the walls that confined me.

When at last I was released I walked out into a cold drizzle. The rain fell onto my cheeks like butterflies resting on my skin. My wrist was freshly bandaged and still ached slightly. We walked to the parking garage and I climbed into the back seat. I watched the hospital through the safety of the windowpane. I watched it as we drove away, craning my neck to count the floors and stare at the windows of the eighth floor. I imagined myself inside looking out and wrapped my arms tighter around myself. Only when the hospital was out of sight did I turn around. I bent forward between the front seats and looked through the windshield until we were home

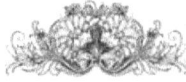

CHAPTER 14

Blog post

I read somewhere that I am thirty times more likely to die than you are.

What do you do with a statistic like that? I tuck it away in the back of my mind. I try not to let it come out to play, to let it run around with its clothes off, naked and flailing. I've been hospitalized twice since all this started. Days of my life have been spent on the inside of hospital walls. Nights alone. It's not fun...but no one said it was going to be.

What do you do with a statistic like that? You try to tune it out, to change the frequency, the station, to something more lively. You don't want to be a statistic, so you take your medicine like a good girl. There, there, swallow it down now. You are vigilant of your symptoms.

What do you do with a statistic like that? You try. You try hard, harder, hardest. You read every book there is on the subject. You try alternative medicine. You try to relax while the number breathes down your neck.

What do you do with a statistic like that? You write a blog telling the world that you are afraid of dying too soon, that you aren't done yet, that you have a hell of a lot of living left to do. You tuck yourself in at night and thank God for another day on this Earth. You cry...but you don't give up. It's just a number—thirty times—it's just a number. Sometimes when you read it's higher but you don't pay attention to that because you aren't dying today or tomorrow or ever. You are living. You are alive.

I Am an Owl

Up here on the roof in the dark, I am an owl. I turn my head, tilt my chin, and watch the calm of the neighborhood at two-thirty in the morning. The streetlights cast a soft yellow glow, illuminating the road below in soft circles like the sun on the Earth. The house across the street is perfect even now in the dark, maybe especially so. The green house is black and the white trim gray. Two steps up from the straight sidewalk is a porch, inviting me over. I think of the children tucked into their beds. I imagine the girl lying in a lavender room and the boy in a blue one. I can see their small faces, still unaware of what it means to regret, to be scarred. Innocent. I see them as though peering through the windows of their gingerbread house.

This is the fifth night in a row that I have climbed out the window and up to the top of the third-story roof. The breeze is warm and soft on my skin, like the whisper of a lover. I can still smell the grass cut when the sun was high and hot. It reminds me of my childhood, cheerleading at soccer games and lying in the grass, watching the clouds roll by. I wish that life were that simple again. I wish to lie in the soft grass, hands behind my head, and make out the shapes in the clouds, see the answers in the sky. I look up at the dark, cloudless night, the ground far below me. There are no answers now.

I sit so high from the ground up here, as this owl in the night, higher than the trees in the backyard, higher than my sleeping parents below. And although I am up here, I am not high enough. I long to be a star. I want to see the world below me. I want to be part of the heavens.

The house below me is wood, painted a light blue, and is a ghost in the moonlight. It's all angles and vaulted ceilings and a chimney to my left. I could sit safely on the deck on the second floor. It would make sense to go out there and sit at the tiny, wrought iron table in a chair made for the outdoors. But sense is something I don't have right now. Sense got carried away in the wind the moment I stepped out my window.

Sometimes I am aware of what I am doing or what I want so desperately to do. In this awareness I am conscious of the danger. I know I shouldn't be climbing on roofs at two o'clock in the morning. When I know this, I call my boyfriend. He tells me not to come up here, that it isn't safe. I try to listen, to heed his warnings. And sometimes I succeed. I stay inside my room, feet firmly planted.

"I want to go on the roof," I say when I call him late at night.

"Am I with you?" he asks me.

"No."

"Then are you allowed to go up there?"

"No. But I really want to," I say. "I need to."

"But it's not safe to go up there alone. You have to wait 'til I'm there," he says. "Then we can go up there together."

I am silent.

"Babe? You know I love you," he says. "I just don't think it's a good idea for you to go out on the roof right now."

"Okay," I tell him, doubting the word as it moves past my lips.

I try to listen, but sometimes I can't hear his voice. I climb out my window, one foot then the other, out onto the steep slope, and forge my way to the spine of the house. I have forgotten his voice tonight, the one warning me away from my perch. The urge was too strong, my will too weak.

He's lying to me. My boyfriend is lying about coming up here together. Part of me believes him that he will come and hold my hand as we climb but the other part of me knows that this will never happen. He is telling me this to stop me. It works sometimes, his logic. It's a trick and I let him blindfold me. I feel the scratch of the fabric on my face. I open my eyes and see nothing. This is an allowance I make when I am conscious of what is real and what is not. But sometimes I can't keep my promise. I can't keep my feet on what is solid. There are times I must try to get high, higher, highest. I am not meant to stand; I am meant to fly.

This is my mania. I lose all inhibition, forget about consequences. There is no ground below, only sky above. I want what I want and nothing else matters. I can't think because the lines turn to circles and black turns to white. I have no fear of falling; if I were slightly more manic I might try to fly. I would spread my wings in the air and let go. I would step off my perch and glide on the breeze as it lifts me up, up. I'd fly over to the neighbor's house and tap on the little girl's window and see if she wants to come out and play. Maybe she could fly too, with the touch of my hand, and we would circle the neighborhood in the night. But my mind hasn't been carried quite that far away.

For the past year and a half, I have lived with my parents. I have moved with them from our home in Oklahoma to this one here in North Carolina. I've been given the third floor of the house. One large room and one smaller. It is like having a studio apartment again, like the one in Manhattan or the one in Austin, only this time it doesn't belong to me. I'm better but I'm still not well. And though I have depressive episodes I am able to get out of bed. I sit at breakfast with my parents. I go for walks with my dog. It is mania that is now my stalker. I am at risk of falling, from the roof, from this life. Falling.

I can't sit still any longer, staring at the lonely street. I stand up. I wonder what I look like from below, standing here on the peak of the roof. I bend at the knees and make my way back to my window. I lose my footing and slide on my butt. My palms are scraped from the rough sandpaper of the shingles. I smile. My window is close and I scoot over to it and climb over the sill. Inside, I sit down at my desk and turn on my computer. I go to my website and type away at my blog. Tip, tap, tip, tap. I am so creative. I am on fire. Burn, baby, burn. Every thought I have is fantastic. Every word I write is golden, shining even in the darkness. I am untouchable.

I wish the world would wake up. I want to talk, to share all my brilliant thoughts. I consider calling my boyfriend. He will listen as I talk in circles and tangents and spheres. He will listen to me for hours. He often does. But he has to work in the morning and he has a life of his own, miles from mine. There is a limit

to my selfishness.

I think about waking up my mom. We could watch a movie if I could sit still, but I can't and we won't. No, I will let her sleep, floors beneath me, next to my father. They are on standby, my boyfriend and mother, for nights like tonight, nights when I am not sleeping. But to wake them would be to admit that something is wrong. I don't want to be wrong. I want to be right.

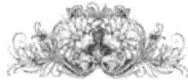

CHAPTER 15

Blog post

It's 5:25 in the morning and I've been up for more than an hour. My sleep pattern is out of whack once again. Ah, the joys of medication. Chemicals meant to work on the brain do so to such an effective extent it is scary. I'm having trouble writing this, having trouble making the words get in the right order, making them grab their jackets and get in a single-file line. "Please. A–K in the front. L–Z in the rear." No one is listening. Everyone is twirling around the middle with his or her arms held wide at their sides. This is your brain on drugs.

So as my new regimen is increasing so too are my side effects. There are the usual—I get really sleepy. Saturday evening I passed out at 6:30pm. I woke up sometime around midnight and took my medicine, went back to bed until my alarm went off at 6am. I thought I was dying when I tried to trudge through my shower. It was like moving my arms while being wired to the ground. I nearly gave up getting ready at one point, quite literally almost threw in the towel. I was just too tired. I knew it was a medicine-induced state; I'd been there before and know how it feels, how it differs from other feelings of sickness or weariness. I've been there more than I can count, so I just kept moving. If you can just get through it, can let it wear off, you'll be okay. I aimed for okay and towel-dried my hair.

An all-too-familiar side-effect has taken residence in my head, sitting down behind the control board of my vocabulary. I can't find the right words. I can't tell you, dear reader, the number of misspelled or misused words that were typed in this passage alone. For instance, you were just a moment ago a "deer" reader. Sorry.Xoxo

Body versus Mind

If you ever want to gain twenty or thirty pounds, might I suggest getting on some mood-stabilizers with a side of antidepressants? Antipsychotics will work, too. Maybe an anticonvulsant? Just swallow them down, or stick them between your cheek and your gum as they melt. Ingest them and the pizza and the chips and the cereal and the mashed potatoes and all the other carbs you eat in an effort to satisfy your insatiable hunger.

Back in 2008, after my suicide attempt and hospitalization, I was put on Zyprexa, an atypical antipsychotic. The little pills went to work changing the chemistry of my brain, tranquilizing me, blocking receptors in the dopamine pathways. At night, hours after going to sleep, I would migrate to the kitchen and prepare a snack. Cereal. Ice cream. Spoon to mouth. Spoon to mouth. And although I barely remembered my nightly treks to the fridge, the evidence was always there in the morning. Empty bowls. Snack cake wrappers. Whoops, I forgot to put the milk back.

In just over a month I gained twenty pounds. It was quite incredible.

For the first year and a half after my diagnosis it was a constant flux of prescription drugs. Zyprexa wasn't quite right. Neither was the Lithium or the Geodone or the Trazadone or the Clorazepam or the Neurontin or the Luvox or the Xanax or the Zoloft or the Cymbalta or the Trileptal or the Seroquel. If there was a drug to treat bipolar disorder and anxiety, at some point, I took it. I needed a pill organizer just to keep track of what to take and when. We were searching for the right combination to stabilize my extreme moods, to subdue the anger and irritability, to help me get up every day but not too high up—we had to avoid mania. And then there was the anxiety, the never-ending fear that haunted me. We'd give the pills a few weeks or months. We had to wait and see if there was an improvement and these kinds of medications take time to work. Give it time, Elaina. Give it time. Then, once my body became comfortable with the cocktail, when I stopped throwing up or getting dizzy or sweating but my moods showed no improvement, we would change the drugs.

I was perpetually hungry.

A year and a half after my first hospitalization, my psychiatrist introduced me to Saphris, another atypical antipsychotic. This drug, when coupled with Lamictal, an anticonvulsant used in bipolar patients as a mood stabilizer, provided me with stability for the first time since my diagnosis. The problem with Saphris was that it made me hungry. All the time. I gained five pounds in the first week. Having been through this side effect before, I was scared of the pounds to come. I talked to my psychiatrist and he put me on Topamax, another anti-seizure medication, the same one my boyfriend's daughter takes for her epilepsy. He prescribed it to curb my appetite and it did. It didn't cause me to lose weight, instead it simply balanced my crazy appetite.

But seven months later I lost my health insurance and Topamax was just one more medication I couldn't afford.I didn't notice the weight as it crept back on. It was silent. Slow, but steady. Over the course of the next year I gained twenty-five pounds. My jeans didn't fit. I couldn't zip up that sexy little black dress my boyfriend loved. It seemed like a hefty price to pay.

Acne. I was twenty-nine with the blemishes of a fifteen year old. I tried everything. Benzoyl peroxide. Salicylic acid. Scrubs. Creams. Lotions and potions. Infomercial miracle cures. Nothing worked.

"I don't want to come this weekend," I said to my boyfriend. I had been planning to drive the four hours from my apartment in Wilmington, North Carolina, to his place in Virginia.

"Why? What's wrong?" he said.

"I just, I feel so ugly. My skin is disgusting."

"Babe, come on. I don't care about your skin; I care about you."

"I just look so ugly. This is ridiculous. I am a grown woman. I shouldn't have a pizza face."

"Please come. I don't care. I think you are beautiful," he said. "I just want to see you."

It was only after my medications changed—again—that my skin cleared. It was such a marked improvement that people asked me what I had done. As happy as I was to once again have a clear complexion, the acne had been so severe that it scarred my cheeks, leaving pockmarks and red spots. Another battle wound in the war with bipolar disorder.

There were other side effects that came and went as we cycled through the pharmacy trying to find the right cocktail. One of the most aggravating ones was the shaking in my hands. The same signature I had had since I was a child became a jerky mess written both above and below the line. I'd been wearing eyeliner and mascara for over a decade and suddenly it was impossible to put them on.

A year after my diagnosis of bipolar disorder, I was taking six different medications. Antipsychotics. Antidepressants. Sedatives. I think it was the sheer number and strength of the drugs that caused a new side effect—double vision. Instead of seeing two headlights going my direction while driving at night, I saw four. Instead of one median, there were two. It was too dangerous to drive. I was back to depending on everyone else to cart me around. When I moved from Oklahoma to North Carolina my new psychiatrist tapered off some of the medication and the double vision went away. I haven't experienced it since.

Today I get regular blood tests to see if the medications I take are damaging my liver. So far, so good. It stands to reason that drugs strong enough to affect the functioning of my brain are also strong enough to affect my other organs. The tests reveal that I now have elevated cholesterol levels due to one of my medications.

At times I've been fatter and I've been uglier. I've been shaky and blind. I've been sick to my stomach and had ferocious headaches. But given the choice of whether or not to take medication for my illness, I would choose medication every single time. Because, you see, the alternative is madness and I've been mad. It isn't fun. I know why I can't seem to shake these extra pounds and I know why the skin on my cheeks is scarred. I know that it is not my fault, that it is simply a price I pay to think clearly. I know that when I swallowed those tiny pills I made a deal—you can have my body if you will just give me back my mind. It was a deal and the pills kept up their end.

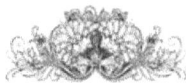

CHAPTER 16

Blog post

Some of you know, some of you don't, but I'm ill. And this isn't the sniffles or stomach flu we are talking about, more like life and death. It isn't all that comfortable for me to talk about so I won't get into the specifics here, if you know me, if you've been close, then you already know.

In my life, I have tried hard to be there for my friends. Through their breakups, fights with lovers, fights with parents, shitty jobs, mean bosses, bad dates, car accidents, sickness and health. I've done my best to listen, to advise when asked, to try as best I can to make things better, or admit when I can't but comfort them with my love.

So I have been shocked and...disappointed doesn't even cover it...by the disappearance of those who I considered my friends. This has been a hard time for me, perhaps the hardest of my life, and I admit most of the time I'm not up for talking, for pretending life is peachy and sunlit and silver-lined. But I don't doubt that feeling loved or at least remembered would help. Since my hospital stay nearly two months ago I've received a handful of calls, and I mean that literally; I could count them on one hand. Even a "Hey, how are you? I've been thinking about you" email would mean some-thing. But truthfully, I got nothing.

My only friends are my family. Writing this brings tears to my eyes because I never would have imagined that my friends would treat me this way, or rather, not treat me at all. One of my best friends called me while I was in the hospital and that's it. That's that. Nothing more.

Again, I realize that through this all I have pushed my friends away, tried to save them from having to deal with my problems. But when the time came, and I thought it was clear that I asked for help, for compassion, for someone to just listen to me, well, it's all fallen on deaf ears.

Those I considered my closest friends, people who would always support me and be there when I needed them, don't give a fuck, and that has weighed heavy on my mind. And I am left to think that I don't matter, not like I should, not like I deserve, not like I need.

I am forced to go it alone because I cannot allow myself this disappointment again. I'll lean on my family, whose love has proved unconditional. I'm not writing this to ask you for help or to be there or to tell you what you should have done. I'm writing this to tell you how on top of being sick, you've broken my heart without saying a word, not a damn word.

Her Arms

I don't mean to ruin things.

In my late twenties, something happened. The crazy came. The madness came. A storm blew in and took with it parts of my mind. I haven't been able to tell if all of it has returned. How do you know what you don't know? How can you remember bits of yourself you have forgotten?

I had a best friend. We met in high school in Ohio. During college we spent a summer together in a rough neighborhood of Brooklyn as we completed internships in Manhattan, then our first year after graduation in New York City. She slept on my couch for six months when she moved down to Austin after I did. She knew me. She knew me. She hated all the guys I dated because they weren't good enough. She loved me that much. She was my plus-one to Austin's VIP events. I was an assistant editor for a local lifestyle magazine and she worked at Waterloo Records. She introduced me to good music. We spent Friday nights listening to live bands, clutching whiskeys, and Saturday mornings talking about guys, holding coffee mugs. We were silly together and made up songs as we walked around downtown Austin. She could make me laugh until my face hurt and she had the best hugs. She would hold me tight in her long arms and squeeze as if to say, "I won't let you fall. I will keep you safe." We knew where we were going. Up. Up. Up.

Bipolar disorder is a mental illness—a mood disorder. It seems so simple but it isn't. Don't be fooled. Bipolar disorder = two words. Mental illness = two words. Mood disorder = two words. But how do you fit a life into two words?

I pushed her away before the first break from reality. Before I drove halfway across the country to California. Before I tried to kill myself. Before my life could be explained by two words.

She tried to help me before I left Austin. She called my mother in Oklahoma and told her to come. She didn't know what to do about the cutting and the bandages and the blood. Her hugs couldn't keep me safe anymore. My smile had become temporary.

She had a new job working for the South by Southwest Music Festival—a dream job—and I had needs. I needed more and more and more. It was unrealistic. The hole had grown and I was trying to fill it. With her. With attention. With everything.

In the psych ward of Mills-Peninsula Hospital in San Mateo, California, after my suicide attempt, she called me. Her words were soft and careful. I could feel her arms through the phone. They wrapped around me and held me, but nothing would ever be right again.

I don't mean to ruin things but I do. I pushed my best friend away because she couldn't be who I needed her to be. She grew busy. I was dying and she couldn't come with me. I had to push her away. I loved her that much.

I never had another friend like her. Not before. Not after.

Perhaps it is like a first love; it lingers in the dark corners of your heart and the sun hits your face and that song comes on and you smile and then you cry and you wish life was different. You wish you didn't know those two words. You wish they were part of someone else's story or a made-for-TV movie or something you learned in Psych 101 or just an abstract thought. You don't want to know what it feels like to only see your family during visiting hours. You don't want to know about vitals and bad decaffeinated coffee. You don't want to have to put the pale pink roses your mother brought in a plastic cup on the floor by your bed in the room you share with an ancient lady because they can't trust you with glass. You don't want to remember what it felt like to dance to the music of one of your favorite Austin bands and sweat and shimmy and shake and laugh with your best friend because she is gone now.

I ruined it.

"It's okay, Elaina. You don't have to apologize," she said. But it's not and I can't. It was out of my control. My mind doesn't work like hers. Sometimes my mind doesn't work at all. I live in this weird world where I forget nearly everything. Maybe that is for the best. Who wants to remember the time she met me for coffee at an outdoor café and I cried and she made me believe everything would be okay? Who wants to remember the subway rides and those hot summer afternoons we spent at the museum? Who wants to remember being so poor we barely scraped by but were happier than we had ever been?

Angry words are a solvent. They break down everything you have built. I pushed. She pulled.

We don't speak. Every once in a while a text will be shared and we will pretend that we are going to. We pretend that what is gone isn't really gone. We pretend that we know each other, but we don't. We haven't spoken in years. I can't tell you who she's dating; I used to know his favorite drink.

I am not bitter. This is not bitterness. This is longing. This is missing something. This is wishing I had her to tell me who I used to be—before the madness, before my life became two words.

So I must be thankful—for her and the sanity I used to know. I lump them together. They fall under the "Before" heading. Today is "After." It is mood stabilizers and antipsychotics and antidepressants and psychiatrists and therapists. It is "used to be" and "once upon a time." It is the three pair of hospital socks in the top drawer. It is wishing I could remember and wanting to forget.

I don't mean to ruin things, but I can't help it. My mind wanders away and my words decide what will come out and how fast and how hard. They need. They push. There is no forgiveness.

I'd like to tell her I am sorry. I would like to tell her I didn't mean it when I told her not to call me anymore. But as I said, angry words are a solvent. They dissolved what we had a long time ago. Memories are left, pictures in which we smile at the camera, unaware of who I will become, pictures of when we were happy, pictures of her arms around me.

CHAPTER 17

Blog post

Be Brave, Elaina J.

You wouldn't know it by looking at me. You wouldn't hear it in my laugh or smell it on my skin. It wouldn't announce itself like a suitor at the door a century ago. When I tell you about the time I styled The Real World: Austin cast or if you heard me on the radio you wouldn't have a clue. I chain words together to form sentences. I lasso sentences around the moon. You wouldn't know it by looking at me, but I am sick.

I am mentally ill.

It has something to do with chemicals and my brain. Too little. Too much. It has to do with stress and life. It is no one's fault, not yours.

Not mine.

I have obsessive compulsive disorder. And anxiety disorder. And one upon a time post-traumatic stress disorder. But most importantly, I have bipolar disorder.

I didn't catch it like a bad cold. It must have always been there, waiting. Breathing on my neck. Sitting in the dark. It waited until I was flying high to make me crash. And unlike a cold, it won't go away. Ever.

I have bipolar disorder and it has changed my life. It has taken my career and some of my friends. It has broken relationships. It has broken my heart. It has led me to the Intensive Care Unit, the psych ward, free clinics, Duke University, and more doctors than I can name.

Up to a third of all people who have bipolar disorder die by their own hand. Suicide. Death. I have nearly died. A few times. When my mind is right it is not there, that dark shadow. But sometimes I lose my mind. I climb trees in sequined dresses. I go 110 mph. I climb on third-story roofs at two in the morning. There is more. So much more. But those are secrets for me and those that love me.

By telling you this, dear reader, I risk turning you away. But I am stable now. I take my medication. I go to therapy. I see a psychiatrist. I manage.

I am telling you because I need to be honest. I want to talk about the mentally ill. I want to be okay with myself. I don't want to hide anymore. My mental illness is a part of me, as much a part as my curly hair and green eyes.

There is a stigma attached to the mentally ill. If I had heart disease or diabetes people would sympathize, make exceptions. But because my illness affects my mind, it is seen in a different light. I cannot be trusted. Words from my mouth are shaken with salt.

I am writing my experience in words and pages and chapters. I want to share it with you. Bring you inside the hospital walls, take you up on the roof. I want you to understand how it feels to not trust yourself, to check in every day and make sure that your mind is indeed still there. It's scary. I am scared most of the time.

I have grown dependent—on my family, on my boyfriend, on my best friends. They hold me down, keep me from flying into the sky. They watch me through trained eyes. Am I well? Am I sane?

I want to make it okay. I want to write my way into your heart so that when you hear the phrase "mentally ill" you open your arms, you say, "I don't understand, but I will listen to you," you say, "I know Elaina J. and she is sick but she is beautiful."

I wouldn't be who I am without my illness. It has shaped me;

created a curve in the J.

And I am so blessed. I have people who care about me, who take care of me when I can't, I have my words and sentences and essays. I have a way to speak when my mouth is closed. I have you, dear reader.

I don't want to hide anymore. I don't want to be embarrassed or ashamed. I don't want to pretend that everything is okay when it isn't. I don't want to lie, white or otherwise. I don't want to stretch the truth to fit me. I want to be me. Bipolar disordered me. Mentally ill me. Me.

I could say I would understand if you stopped reading or stopped calling, but I wouldn't. I am still me, just a little more quirky than most. I am still me, just with an excuse for what you can't understand.

I have made mistakes. Haven't you? Fueled by mania I have lost my mind. A lot. But I always come back, sometimes quicker than others. I forget what I've said and what I've done and I ask you to remind me. Psychotic breaks. Mental amnesia. Just another day as ElainaJ.

I've been holding off on posting this blog for a while now. I am afraid—of what you will say, of what you will do. But I need to be okay with who I am, whether you like me or not...and I am okay. A little bit crazy. A lot of bit kind.

I hope you'll stay.

xoxo,

Elaina J.

Is Anybody There?

With my illness came changes—to the relationships I had, to the relationships I would build. Before the madness came I trusted few people. I didn't want to be disappointed, to be hurt. But when you are sick, when you nearly lose your life, you realize that you must trust others because you can no longer trust yourself.

I learned to listen to my doctors—psychiatrists and therapists. Surely they had the answers, the cure, the hope. I took their pills. I told them my secrets—how I wanted to die, how I wanted to live. I called their emergency numbers when the screaming in my head wouldn't stop. I sat on their couches, their upholstered chairs, a big desk between us. Doctor. Patient. I let them shoot medicine in my hip, something to bring me back down. I tried to believe they could save me.

I learned to trust my boyfriend. It wasn't easy. Although he wasn't the first guy I dated after Ashton, he was the first boyfriend to whom I made a commitment. I let him learn the curves of my body. I let him walk around the inside of my mind. I let him stop the bleeding and take me to the emergency room when I overdosed. What I wrote I read to him. What I feared, I shared.

"How can I be a mother when I might have to go into a psych ward again? Every time I go it is for a longer stay. What would my baby think when her mother disappears? Or when she is older how do I explain it? And what happens on those days when I am too depressed to get out of bed? Or what if I am manic and do something crazy?" I said. "I don't know how I can do it."

"Babe, I will be here. I will help. Your mom will help. If you want a baby, we can have a baby. I know you would be a great mother. Don't let this stop you."

"But I would have to go off my medication and take something safer for a pregnancy. These meds work. I don't want to switch and, to be honest, I don't want to take anything while I am pregnant. And if I am not on my meds I will get depressed and manic and that will put not only me but our baby at risk. And then there is the possibility that our child could have bipolar disorder. I wouldn't wish this on anyone," I said. "I couldn't bear to see my child go through what I have had to go through."

"Babe, we'll figure it out. I love you," Jeremy said.

When I am depressed I am ugly and dark. I don't want anyone to see me. I don't want them to see that I can't get dressed. I don't want them to smell my breath with teeth unbrushed. I am hopeless and my friendships become hopeless. I don't have the energy to raise the phone to my ear, to move my lips. I spend my time curled up in bed staring into space. I decline invitations. I don't answer emails. I withdraw from the world. I sleep days and nights away. I close like a book. The sun disappears and I cannot navigate the darkness. All seems lost and so I lose. Friends drift away. The phone calls become less and less frequent until they stop altogether. The invitations I turned down no longer arrive. I pick fights. I tell my best friend not to call me anymore and so she doesn't. I lose her forever.

There is no instruction book on how to treat a suicidal woman. You must fumble along and hope to say the right thing. Please, God, don't let me say the wrong thing. My best friend from college calls me in the hospital and I tell him I tried to kill myself. I failed, I say. He asks why I wanted to die and I tell him I don't know because I don't. He takes my words and turns them over in his head with awkward hands. "I'm sorry," he says. That is all he says and the line becomes silent. I wonder if he is still there and then I hear him cough. He tells me to feel better, to call if I need anything. Then he is gone.

I am still hesitant to say the words "mental illness" or "bipolar disorder" to people I meet. What will they think if they know I am crazy? What will they say when I disappear into the hospital for weeks at a time? I am afraid they will go away, that they won't want to be my friend. After all, people I thought loved me went away. Why would these new friends choose to stay?

People who know about my mania and how it is often brought on by stress are careful with me. They don't tell me things that might scare me. Our relationships have become unbalanced. I share everything, but they are selective. Don't overwhelm her. Careful, careful.

I have learned a different kind of honesty. I have few secrets. Between my therapist, my psychiatrist, my friends, my family, and my boyfriend there is always someone to talk to. When my head starts to buzz and I talk twice as much as I normally do—signs that mania is just around the corner—I tell my boyfriend; I call my mom. I ask them to keep an eye on me. I expect them to help keep me safe. I cannot trust myself so I must trust them.

When I admitted to my illness on my blog I was unsure of what to expect. How would I be judged? What would people say to me or about me? I was pleasantly surprised. People offered to listen to me when I needed them. A friend that I had been having weekly coffee with for a few months but who didn't know about my diagnosis offered to climb trees and rooftops with me when I was manic. People talked about my strength and my courage and my heart. They told me they loved me and this made me trust a little more. Perhaps it was okay to be me, disordered, mentally ill–me.

Those who were left after I became ill were those who mattered. They accepted me for who I was, not for who I had been. My relationships deepened as I became more honest, more open. I learned what love meant. It meant being there for 2am phone calls. It meant bringing clean underwear to the hospital. It meant emergency rooms and blood and pills. But it also meant my smile and the crinkles around my eyes. It also meant laughing with me when I was bouncing off the walls, rolling your eyes when I was up a tree, and holding my hand as I bared my soul to the world. I learned it was okay to be imperfect. I could look in my photo album and remember what it felt like before the madness came, but I could also look forward to the adventures that lie ahead. So I wouldn't always be stable, so sometimes I would be a little crazy, who the fuck cared? People loved me and supported me and I was amazing, just as I was.

I realized I couldn't live my life feeling ashamed for the chemistry in my brain. I would be honest with people. My mental state is intrinsic to who I am, as much as my curly hair or the brown-green color of my eyes. Hiding it made me feel embarrassed and damaged and unworthy.

My relationship with God changed too. I was raised a Christian in the United Methodist Church. I attended Sunday school. I went through confirmation. I was the youth group president. I loved my God. I talked to him often. We had a close relationship.

After my suicide attempt I was so angry with God. Why did you abandon me? You turned your back and in that moment you let me slip and fall. I blame you, God. You let this happen. You forgot about me. I have always been faithful. I have always shared your love, prayed, believed. Where was your faith in me?

When I nearly died, I changed. I was not the same person I was before. That person was gone. I was now a new person, a person I didn't know, a person I didn't recognize. When I came to, when a part of my mind returned, it returned to a different Elaina. This new one was scared and lonely and sad. The new me no longer believed in an ever-present God. I felt like he had failed me.

For months I gave him the silent treatment. I thought about my near death a lot. If my roommate hadn't found me that night, I would be dead. What would my family have done? How could I have done this to them? What if I try again? One day I was thinking about it and about God and how I felt. What if you didn't turn your back at all; what if I was alive because you saved me; what if you were there the whole time, watching me try to kill myself; what if while I was lying on the linoleum in the kitchen, you were there cradling my head?

The more I thought about these things the more they made sense. This was the God I had believed in all my life, a God of compassion and love. The God I had always believed in wouldn't turn his back. He would save me. I bowed my head and folded my hands and prayed.

God, thank you. I understand now. I am here because you saved me. You sent my roommate to the kitchen. You guided the EMTs' hands and those of the doctors and nurses in the ICU to save me. Only you know when my time is up, not me. Forgive me for being so careless with my life. Please protect me and keep me safe. Please don't let me lose my mind again. Please. Amen.

I questioned God. Why me; why must I suffer; why was so much I worked to build taken away? Most of the time he didn't give me an answer. I looked at the picture I got for confirmation when I was a teenager: The will of God will never lead you where the grace of God cannot keep you. I wondered if that were still true.

I prayed every night, sometimes throughout the day. Thank you, God, for my stability. Thank you for giving me a sound mind today. Please make me sane tomorrow; don't let me lose my mind again. Give me the strength to face tomorrow, whatever it brings. Forgive me for being reckless with my life. Forgive me for hurting myself. Please let those I have hurt forgive me. Thank you for my life. Thank you for being there through the overdoses, the slitting of my wrist. Thank you for keeping me from falling from the roof those nights and for making sure I didn't wreck my car when I was manic. Thank you for giving me another day.

Mental illness changes everything—who I was and how everyone treated me. There was a purpose I felt to live my life feeling okay with myself, to be honest and to trust. It was a crazy life filled with highs and lows and regrets, but it was also beautiful. It was my pass to be a little bit more than normal—a little more creative, a little more compassionate, a little more brave.

CHAPTER 18

Blog post

I took a break. A while ago, I took a break. I'd done a lot. Accomplished. Working hard, hard, harder. Traveling. Late nights. Weekends. Being there. Being on. Shining bright. I was Superwoman. And then I crashed into the ocean. Ripples. Earthquakes. Rubble. I was scooped up and held close and for the first time in a long time I took a deep breath. I slept; for a long time I slept. I don't remember my dreams, only the nightmares, but Superwoman doesn't forget how it felt to fly.

Recently, I woke up. I'm stretching, wiping the sleep from my eyes. I remember where I've been, what I've done. My muscles have atrophied; I can't fly, not yet. But I'm ready now, I've had my break. I'm ready for the next chapter. I want to be.

Enough

"I'm Elaina and I'm an addict."

I sat there at the twelve-step Alcoholics Anonymous meeting with ten addicts and alcoholics. A near-lethal Xanax overdose brought me in. It started a month or two earlier; my downhill spiral, my cries for help. I was taking Xanax at the first flutter of anxiety, not wanting to be left alone with the feeling, the screaming inside my own head, the itch I couldn't scratch. I had become my own pharmacist, every now and again taking more than my allotted milligram. Sometimes three, sometimes five pills. Ten.

One morning I woke up with a medicated hangover. My speech slurred and my feet dragged as if I had had one too many cocktails. I told my boyfriend I had taken pills the night before. A look of disappointment showed on his face. He let me go back to sleep. When I woke up that afternoon we went out—coffee and a bagel. He told me my mom had sent him a text message asking if I was all right. Apparently I had called my cousin Kimberly the night before, crying into the phone. She had talked to my mom that morning and told her that she was worried. I didn't remember the conversation.

We sat silently chewing.

"We need to talk about something," Jeremy began. I knew where he was going.

"You need to be careful with the pills," he said. "You are taking pills you don't need to take. It isn't good."

I did what I always did. I quit talking. I avoided his eyes and looked everywhere else; the floor, the space behind his head, inside. For the rest of the day I stayed quiet, mad at him for putting a magnifying glass on the problem. When I took a few Xanax everything became fuzzy, easier to digest.

The day after the first time I took ten pills, I hit a parked car. The medication was still in my system, even though it had been hours and hours since I'd washed it down with a glass of cheap white wine, even though I had slept ten hours. I backed out of the driveway to go to the grocery store and bumped into the car parked on the street. It felt slight, a tap, so I didn't get out and check. As I pulled back into the driveway twenty minutes later I did so too closely to the parked trailer, ripping off my passenger-side mirror and gouging the fender. A half an hour later I noticed from my window above the garage that a policeman was standing in my driveway looking at my car. I went outside to face him and noticed my neighbor standing in the street.

"Did you hit this car?" asked the policeman. It was then that I noticed the dent in the fender, the dent I had caused.

"Yes, but I didn't know I had hit it that hard. I thought I just bumped it. I'm sorry," I said to him and the neighbor.

"You know you could be cited for a hit and run for this," he said.

"I'm so sorry," I said. "I didn't realize,"

"You need to exchange insurance information with Ms. George," he said.

I hurried inside and got my insurance card. When I returned the policeman had left me with a mad neighbor.

"I am so sorry," I said as I followed her into her house.

"Let me see your insurance card," she said.

I stood there awkwardly looking around her kitchen, listening to the hum of the refrigerator. She handed the card back to me.

"I really am sorry," I said.

"Yeah."

I turned around, walked out her front door and across the street to my house.

This should have been enough to scare me away from the pills. It wasn't.

It takes the energy of mania to act on the suicidal wishes of the depressed, and I was just this side of manic. I had been depressed for months. Sleep was my escape. There were never enough hours in the night to satisfy my craving for peaceful oblivion. The bed was my sanctuary. The world was gray except when I was with other people, when I was with my boyfriend. With him the sun shone and the birds sang. I saw the blooming flowers where once had been only weeds. Left alone I was miserable. Life had lost its appeal. I joined a gym. I practiced yoga. It took a Herculean effort to get out the door but I knew exercise could help me; my doctor prescribed it along with my mood-stabilizing meds. So I sweated and stretched and prayed to make it through one more day. But death was always there, hiding in the shadows, whispering in the wind.

Life came fast. My aunt, who had taught me to make our family's Hungarian nut roll and always made a coconut cream pie for me during the holidays even though she didn't eat it, the same aunt that I had stood beside as a bridesmaid when she got married, had recently been diagnosed with cancer and everything had moved quickly, far too quickly for me to deal with. She had immediate surgery to remove the tumor that had grown inside her and was now in intensive care at the VA hospital in Oklahoma City fighting to stay alive. I wanted to be with her, to make everything better. I had no control.

Then my boyfriend came home from his lawyer's office. He told me he would be getting his children every weekend. I had been living with him for two months and was still getting used to having them at our home every other weekend. Now they'd be there every weekend? My mind flew through the scenarios. No more weekends alone. No more going out on Friday or Saturday night. No more us. I got on the phone with my girlfriend and told her the news. She shared time with her boyfriend and his daughter and understood. She told me to talk to my boyfriend about how I felt, that I shouldn't stew over it. So I took her advice and told my boyfriend that I valued our time together and that this would change things. Then I sat back on my couch and my one glass of wine turned into two and then three. I began to wash down pills. I felt myself coming apart, like the hold I had on my life wasn't really a hold at all, like I was trying to grab onto a fistful of water. It was like drowning and getting my head above the water only to be sucked back down.

I grabbed sweats and threw them in my suitcase. The world was off kilter. I stumbled to my dresser as my boyfriend slept. It was resting on the floor at a diagonal. I grabbed some hooded sweatshirts and removed the ties. I knew if I went to the hospital I would have to stay and this time I wanted to be prepared. And while I packed I ingested pills, ten at a time. It was early in the morning, still dark out, when I fell into the bedroom and woke up my boyfriend.

He took me and my suitcase to the nearby hospital and fidgeted in his seat in the emergency room waiting area as I dozed in and out until they called my name.

"Babe, I gotta go," he said as he helped me walk to the nurse, pulling my suitcase behind him.

"What? Why? Stay."

"Elaina, I can't, I have to go. The Navy doesn't have sick days," he said. "I am sorry. I would stay if I could. I will call you soon and check on you."

"Okay," I said. "I'm scared."

"Don't be scared. They are going to take care of you," he said. "I will call you soon. I love you."

And then things grew fuzzy. I don't remember the faces of the doctors. I don't remember them dressing me in a hospital gown, placing my clothes in a plastic bag. I don't remember the EKG or the IV going in. But I do remember drinking through a straw a cup of charcoal, the grit, the weight of it on my tongue. I remember my shit black as night. I handed over the card for my psychiatrist to one of the nurses, hoping he could help. I couldn't find my cell phone. I couldn't remember my boyfriend's or my mother's number. My boyfriend called again later that morning. I was asleep the first time. I asked for a piece of paper and wrote down his cell phone number and got my mother's number. I stayed in my hospital gown that day, alone, waiting to be transferred somewhere else. I expected to be taken away to a psychiatric facility. After all, that was what was recommended in the hospital report. "The patient has a bed at Virginia Beach Psychiatric." It was early in the morning, maybe two, maybe five o'clock, when I boarded an ambulance. I was still intoxicated from the mania and the Xanax. I sat on the gurney in the back of the bus as we sped through the darkness.

It's hard to remember what happened through the haze of the fifty or so pills. Mania didn't help. I tend to lose my mind and memory when I am in an episode. I arrived at the Recovery Center, not Virginia Beach Psychiatric, early in the morning. The other patients slept. I remember peeing in a cup and handing it to a man with a long gray ponytail in a baseball hat. Then I sat next to a desk as a man asked me question after question about my life and I incoherently rambled answers. Then somehow I was in a small room on a plastic mattress across from another empty bed. I woke early to a crack of light piercing the black and a voice telling me it was time for vitals. I stumbled into the bright room and sat down as a middle-aged woman with short brown hair took my blood pressure and temperature. Then I went back to bed. I remember very little of the first couple days except that I slept and groggily attended group meetings.

On Monday, three days after my overdose, I woke up.

The Recovery Center was a place for addicts and alcoholics. At first, I balked. I wasn't an addict. I had taken more pills than were necessary from time to time, but I could go days without taking any. As the days wore on I became defeated. I was questioned all day long during group sessions and twelve-step meetings, so I took on the title. I sat at the meetings and recited, "I'm Elaina and I'm an addict."

The Recovery Center was not attached to a hospital. It was a two-story brick building surrounded by a six-foot fence a mile from the beach. The cold from the floors seeped through the issued blue slippers we wore to breakfast and group meetings. The main living area on the second floor served several functions. On one end was a counter behind which sat the staff. A gate divided us from them and we could only pass through it with permission. In front of the counter were tables surrounded by blue plastic chairs. It was here that we sat for vitals every six hours. Our blood pressure and temperature was taken and recorded. Occasionally we would participate in an activity, like coloring. The women would share baskets of crayons while the men attended a men-only twelve-step meeting downstairs. The right third of the room functioned as a living room. There was a small television, leather chairs, and an upholstered couch. We spent a lot of time watching television or old movies on the donated VCR. Sometimes it took us half an hour to vote on what to watch and the decision came only after a democratic vote.

Against the right wall sat a leather chair and an end table topped with a telephone. We could not dial the phone ourselves. We had to hand over the number to a nurse. She dialed the number from the staff station and told the voice on the other end that there was a call for him or her. She transferred the call to the phone and when it rang the patient picked up and carried on his or her conversation. We were allowed one five-minute phone call twice a day. After being in the Center for a few days my phone privileges went up to two ten-minute phone calls. I called my mother and boyfriend every day. Never long enough, the calls reminded me that I belonged to something bigger, something beyond vital signs and twelve-step meetings. Hang in there, Elaina. Their voices were like pleasant sedation.

Surrounding the main living area were the bedrooms. Most rooms housed two or three patients, but there were a couple of singles. The bed on the wall opposite mine went empty for days. I had privacy, a place to escape. On the fifth day I was moved to a room occupied by three other women. I lay awake at night listening to the sound of Melanie snoring and the crackle of plastic when one or another would turn in her sleep.

Off the main living area was a laundry room. The Center provided detergent to use in one of the two washing machines and someone was always waiting to use the only working dryer. Men and women weren't allowed to share the same space without the watchful eye of the staff, this was true for the laundry room as well as the elevator.

The women's bathroom consisted of three toilet stalls, three shower stalls, a counter with two sinks, and a warped metal mirror. Glass was dangerous. We kept a plastic chair in the bathroom and set it outside of the shower so we could keep our clothes and towels off the floor. Surprisingly, the shower water was always warm and the tiles were clean. I was met with a pleasant smell every morning when I opened the bathroom door, as one or more of the women showered with flowery shampoos and body washes behind the blue nylon curtains.

On the first floor was the cafeteria where we stood in line for our meals and then sat at a long table dividing the room. This was also where we sat through long twelve-step meetings and occasionally art therapy. Down the hall, just past the elevators, was a classroom where we sat for hours listening to talks about addiction. It was in this room that we also participated in acupuncture. Two members of the staff were trained to stick thread-like needles into the flesh of our ears. I would sit as still as I could as they bent over my turned head. I would feel a prick, then another. I would turn my head to the other side and feel a few more pricks. After the staff member had gone around the room to the other ten patients, pricking their tender flesh, she would turn the lights off and turn on the meditation music. This was supposed to not only relax us but also help heal us of our addictions.

One by one, we were pulled from group discussions and taken through two sets of locked doors to the offices of the psychiatrists. The office of Dr. Green was void of pictures and plaques. No soft couch to sit on. It was hard for me to appreciate psychiatrists at inpatient facilities. What did they know? What I told them. They had no background. They were dealing with patients in crisis, lots of patients in crisis, so they had neither the time nor the desire to get to know me. And there wasn't enough time. Most medication prescribed took days if not weeks to take effect, so there was no way to see results under their care. The stay was too brief.

"I don't like prescribing Xanax," Dr. Green said. "It is like alcohol in a pill. It has the same effects."

Dr. Green was large, at least six-foot-two. What little hair he had was gray and swept fruitlessly over his bald spot. He breathed loudly through his nose as he studied my file. His suit was too big and his maroon tie was ugly.

"Oh. I've been on it for a long time."

"As you've discovered, it is addictive," he said. "So, you overdosed?"

"Mmm hmm. It wasn't an accident. I was aware of what I was doing."

"Were you trying to kill yourself?"

"No. I don't think so. I think I was just trying to get some help. I've been depressed for months and then all of a sudden there were a lot of stressors. It just all got to be too much."

"So you've been hospitalized before? Twice?"

"Yes. In October of 2008 and then January 2010."

"What happened then?"

"Well, the first time I tried to kill myself by overdosing on Xanax. The second time I cut my wrist."

"This has been rough for you, hasn't it?" Dr. Green asked. He put down my file and looked at me, waiting for an answer.

"Yes, it has. Since the spring of 2007 I have been dealing with this, this madness and yes, it has been rough."

"Are you thinking about killing yourself now?"

"No," I said. "I'm good."

"I'd like to keep you for a week. Give you some time to collect yourself. Maybe learn how to deal with your stress instead of taking the Xanax."

I stared at the blue carpet. Another week of this? The twelve-step meetings. The squabbling over what to watch in the evenings. The vital checks. The bad coffee. The addicts. The alcoholics.

"Really?" I asked.

"I think it is in your best interest, Ms. Martin. I will see you tomorrow and check in on how you are doing."

With that he stood up and came around the metal desk. He opened the door and let me pass through the doorway first. When we came to the first set of locked doors he swiped a card and as if by magic there was a click. He did this again at the second set of doors. We walked down the hallway and I was returned to a class on the stages of grief.

Cory was kind and funny and the type of guy you imagined luck pouring over like a summer rain. He always had a smile on his face, a laugh to share. He was as short as I was, just five foot three. He had done time, a year for something he wouldn't share. It was hard to imagine why anyone so happy, so full of life, would need drugs. He was charming sober. He now dabbled in other drugs. Hard drugs. Illegal drugs. He didn't know when to say when and so he said more.

"I'm doing this for my daughter. My wife is pregnant and I need to kick this habit before she gets here. She deserves that much," Cory said.

"That's very responsible of you," I said.

"I died once. Heroin. I overdosed and they brought me back. I never touched the stuff again."

He looked back at his word puzzle. He spent hours with a pen in his right hand and the word puzzle book pressed out in front of him. He was cute; short, but cute. I could see why someone would fall in love with him, why she would want to have his baby. His blue eyes sparkled when he laughed and his laugh was infectious. I wanted to imagine him in a land of rocking chairs, in a land of pink and white onesies and handmade quilts.

The days passed slowly. I was up at six-thirty for round one of vitals. I stood at the door to the nurses' office and waited for my tiny paper cup of pills. They didn't make me feel like Xanax. They could have been Flintstone vitamins. I took my regular meds to stabilize my mood, with the addition of a multivitamin and Phenobarbital, a drug to stave off the seizures of Xanax withdrawal.

Breakfast was at seven—an instant oatmeal and croissants affair. Back upstairs I took a shower and put on an Oklahoma State sweatshirt or long-sleevedT-shirt with black sweatpants. I didn't care how I looked. Normally I wouldn't leave the house without my makeup perfectly applied, but there I didn't wear any and my hair, which I normally wore straight, curled around my ears. Acne scars left to show. Bags under my eyes. Not pretty enough.

Around nine o'clock the meetings started. We talked about addiction. Always addiction. What were the triggers? What had it cost us? Every once in a while the topic of depression or bipolar disorder would find its way into the conversation, but mostly, it was all about addiction. Each night we had a twelve-step meet-ing: Alcoholics Anonymous or Narcotics Anonymous. We'd read the steps aloud and then we'd talk. Each person was called on to talk about their addiction; everyone had to share. Sitting there amongst the crystal meth and heroin users, Xanax was my drug of choice.

"I'm Shane and I'm an alcoholic."

"Hi, Shane," I said.

"So like I've said, I'm an alcoholic. I've been drinking since I was fifteen. I'm forty. It never really affected my life until about five years ago. I showed up drunk a few times to my job working construction and got fired. I got a DUI a year ago and lost my license. I just found out that my liver is enlarged so, basically, if I don't stop drinking I am in trouble."

If I had to listen to Shane's story one more time I might shove one of the forks from the cafeteria we were sitting in into my ear. I knew all about his DUI, his liver, and his girlfriend.

"Then my girlfriend left me. I told her I would change, but I didn't. I am here because I want to change. I know about the twelve steps and am ready to really do them," he said. "I have attended meetings before, I know the serenity prayer, but I am ready now."

All I could think about was my boyfriend and my couch and his hand holding mine. I didn't belong here.

On my second day there a young woman came in to the AA meeting and sat next to me.

"Hi, I'm Alex," she said as she looked at the group. She left out the part about whether she was an alcoholic or an addict. She simply bowed her head and played with the zipper of her white sweatshirt.

"Hi, Alex," we said, like some sad choir. It was meant to make the speaker feel welcome but it left me feeling embarrassed when it was said to me and I felt dumb saying it to the other ten people in the room as we made our way around the table.

At the end of the meeting we held hands. Alex's were cold and thin. She held on to me as though for her life.

"God grant me the serenity to accept the things I cannot change, courage to change the things I can, and wisdom to know the difference," we echoed.

She kept her lips still.

Alex was a heroin junkie. Older addicts told her she had a bad habit for someone her age and she knew she did. She was beautiful and thin—too thin—she wanted drugs more than she wanted to eat. She spent her first few days sleeping through withdrawal, occasionally coming down to pick at her food like a bird. This was her third trip to the Recovery Center. Each time she swore she was done with drugs; each time she was wrong. Her boyfriend was a junkie as well and the two lived in motel rooms, scoring drugs and sharing needles. Daily phone calls to him had her in tears. He told her he was cleaning up on the out- side but she could hear it in his voice, the heroin talking. She couldn't work, not with a habit like hers, with arms full of tracks, so she panhandled. "Homeless. Anything helps." She talked with pride about making more than one hundred dollars in an hour, but I was not impressed. She was a homeless junkie and I didn't care how much money she could make in an hour, there was no way I would ever want to trade places with her.

She was twenty-two and had been to jail. She told me that it had made her look good, being clean and fed. She said she gained nearly twenty pounds and had an ass and great breasts that were once again gone. She told me how awful it was waking up "dope sick," jonesing for a fix the moment she opened her eyes. Alex had overdosed three times and each time, after she'd recovered, she'd gone back to the needle. She'd forgotten how to live any other way. She didn't know how to quit.

It is hard to be a vegetarian on the inside, when your choice of what to eat is what is set out for you. I came in on a weekend and there was no cook for us, just staff behind the glass partition spooning out food. When they noticed I wasn't eating I told them

I was a vegetarian. For the first couple of days I subsisted on peanut butter and jelly spread across stale bread. On Monday a cook showed up and put out a veggie burger for me. I ate one for lunch and dinner every day for the next week.

It's easy to gain weight when you are locked away. No exercise, just food. Desserts bought at discount, patients helping themselves to two at a time. Unlike my other hospital stays, here sugar was dished out. It helped wean addicts off drugs, gave them a replacement. We drank decaffeinated coffee all day long. It was weak and unpleasant but it was hot and if you closed your eyes, you could pretend it was the coffee you made at home.

Robby was a young guy, younger than me at twenty-four, with shaggy brown hair and a goatee. He was the father of two and an alcoholic. He talked a lot during the Alcoholics Anonymous meetings, sharing his story. He enjoyed the Recovery Center, thrived on its sense of community. He wanted desperately to be a good father, to be a good man, but his drinking was getting in the way.

"One is too many and a thousand is never enough," he said.

"Are you scared about leaving?" I asked him the day before he did.

"Yeah. I mean, I am excited to see my kids but, you know, it's a great big world out there. It's not as easy as it is in here. In here you can stay sober. You have people to help you, people who care about you. The outside is the same as when I left it and there is temptation everywhere. I'm ready to be a new man, but I'm not sure I am ready to leave yet."

When he left the following morning he carried just a small bag of his belongings in his hand. He asked permission from the staff and doled out hugs to many of us. I wanted him to be okay. I wanted him to forget about me. I didn't want him to remember my name or the Recovery Center or the cafeteria or Dr. Green. I wanted him to be better. I wanted him to not be an alcoholic. I wanted what he wanted. When he put his arms around me I experienced a pang of longing. I missed my boyfriend, missed his smell and my hand in his.

Melanie came in as high as the bright blue sky above our building, talking a million miles an hour. This was her second trip to the Recovery Center, her first just weeks prior. She was a pill popper and didn't discriminate on what the pills were. She had had facial reconstructive surgery following the removal of a tumor and was self conscious of the puffiness along the left side of her jaw. She hid behind her hair, running her fingers through it incessantly and drawing it over her face. Doctors had prescribed her pain medication and she had taken advantage of it, downing more and more pills. She would wake up in the morning and swallow twenty-five pills and a Pepsi. All day long she would pop pills, needing few of them, wanting them all.

I had arrived at the Recovery Center on Saturday morning. On Monday a caseworker from the Community Services Board visited me. Rashonda was younger than me and had short black hair and a dazzling smile of white porcelain. I sat on the bed in my room as she brought a plastic chair in from the main living space. She sat awkwardly, rifling through her portfolio.

"I've brought the wrong notebook," she said. "I had some notes and questions prepared but I must have left it on my desk. I'll just have to use this one." She looked over some papers and looked up at me.

"So why are you here?" she asked.

"I took too much Xanax," I said.

"Why did you take too much Xanax?"

"I've been under a lot of stress. I guess it just got to be too much."

"Were you trying to kill yourself?"

"No." I hadn't set out to kill myself. Or had I? I wasn't sure anymore.

"Then what were you trying to do?"

"I needed help," I said.

"Why did you need help?"

"Like I said, I've been under a lot of stress. And I've been depressed."

"It says here you were drinking. Do you drink a lot?"

"No, not a lot."

"So the Xanax, how much do you take?"

"Well, I am allowed three pills a day but sometimes I take them all together instead of spaced out. And a few times I've taken five," I said. She wrote in her notebook and I wondered what it said. That I was an addict? That I wanted to kill myself?

"You mentioned something about your boyfriend and three kids when you came in. What was that about?"

"Oh. That." I was surprised she knew about that. What else had I babbled when I came in, what other secrets had been revealed? "The day I overdosed my boyfriend told me that his kids would be spending every weekend with us instead of every other weekend. It freaked me out."

"What did you say to your boyfriend when he told you that?" she asked me.

"I told him that it would change things, that I valued our time together. I don't remember there being much of a conversation about it."

"So, I'm here to help you," she said. "The Community Services Board sent me here to make sure you are being treated well and that you have a plan for after care. Are you getting anything out of the Recovery Center?"

I thought for a moment. "I'm learning a lot about addiction."

We talked for another fifteen minutes about my plans. Would I attend twelve-step groups? Did I have a therapist? Did I have a psychiatrist? How would I change things? I talked about getting a therapist and getting individual counseling. I'd been without a therapist for three months and it was beginning to show. I told her I would leave Xanax alone. I would try to become acquainted with anxiety, maybe try a different medicine. She handed me her card and told me she'd be back to see me on Wednesday.

Kylie was just twenty-two and tiny, weighing just over one

hundred pounds. At home she woke up to a fistful of pills and lay down at night with unneeded medicine coursing through her veins. Her neighbor was her dealer. Ask and she shall receive. She'd taken more pills than she could name and flipped her car on a Friday night. As she crawled out the window she knew she had hit bottom. On her right leg was a swollen blue bump like a second bruised knee. No more, she swore and found her way to the Recovery Center. Her two-year-old daughter wasn't in the car when it had turned over on that stretch of road but that was all she could think of—what if? I didn't understand her. How could she be so cute and small and care about her makeup and her hair and be so fucked up? Didn't she care about her daughter? How the hell did she take care of her baby girl when she was high as a kite, everyday, all the time? Didn't she care about herself? In group she talked about her mother, a crack addict. She cried over her daughter and the mother she had become, much like her own.

Rashonda came back on Wednesday as promised. She again asked me what I was getting out of the experience and my answer was the same: I was learning a lot about addiction. She told me that the Community Service Board had psychiatric care available for those without insurance. I would be starting Medicare the following month, so it was determined that those services would not be available to me. I was on my own.

George wore a fool's goofy grin. His years with the bottle and countless cigarettes had given him a gravelly voice and wrinkles. He laughed often and told the same jokes over and over. Time had not been good to George. The alcohol had rotted more than his gut. His trip to the Recovery Center was a time of respite. Here he was given warm meals and a bed to sleep in. When he left, he left for the streets. No home. No family. A hard life welcomed him back like a punch in the face.

And so there I was, mixed up with all these characters and others like them. Unlike with my previous hospitalizations, I didn't belong at the Recovery Center. I had a problem with Xanax, but I wasn't an addict. I looked around at people who had lost their children, their licenses, and their jobs and thought

Enough. That is enough. I had lost so much to my illness I wasn't willingly going to lose more. What I needed was a psychiatric facility, a place with therapy, a place where we talked about feelings, not drinking and drugs.

I stayed in the Recovery Center for nine long days. In the weeks following my release it all seemed like a bad dream. The people I had met were ghosts. I had seen what alcohol could do, how it could ruin lives. I knew I had to be careful with it, too. I knew I had to maintain control. I no longer filled my Xanax prescription and when I saw my psychiatrist a week later I told him not to write me any more. This had been my second overdose and I couldn't trust myself not to make that mistake again. When I told my doctor how many pills I had taken he put down my file and looked me in the eye.

"Elaina, that could have killed you. That is enough to stop your breathing."

Once again I had nearly taken my own life. My psychiatrist's words kept me up at night. I laid on my boyfriend's chest in the dark, listening to his breathing, knowing that I very easily might not have been there. I imagined my parents and the pain my death would cause. I thought of my desk sitting there waiting for me to write. For every bit of me that wanted to die there was a part that wanted to live. I wanted it to get better. I wanted to greet the morning instead of fearing it. I wanted to get out of the house instead of hiding in it. Life was tough, but I was strong, stronger than the little peach pills and cheap white wine. I never wanted to sit through another twelve-step meeting. I didn't want my blood pressure and temperature taken regularly. I never again wanted to sleep on a plastic mattress with rough sheets and a blanket that was never warm enough. I never again wanted to see my face distorted in a warped metal mirror in a community bathroom.

Enough. That is enough.

CHAPTER 19

Blog post

My last visit to the hospital cost me. I got the bill last week and the number reflected proves more than my bank account holds. This is not a good place to be. I've been here before. I know things will work themselves out. I now know they cannot, in fact, take my firstborn child. They just want some money. So I called up the hospital's billing office and asked if there was financial assistance. There is! I've filled out the required form, attached proof of income and bank statement, and am faxing that baby out this morning. I don't know what will happen. Maybe they will put me on a payment plan, maybe they will reduce my bill; anything helps. My health insurance starts today. If only I'd have gotten sick while insured. Sigh. You just can't plan these things, can you? So now I have this big bill to contend with and my health to resurrect. It may take some time.

Every Penny Counts

Being bipolar comes with a cost. For every high, there is a low. It takes and it takes and when it is done, it takes some more. It drains more than emotions; it drained my resources. There was a career and money and time and it took them all. It took my dignity, as I lay in hospital beds under the watchful eyes of nurses. It took my mind.

After my suicide attempt, everything changed. There followed a depression unlike any I had ever known, and getting out of bed became nearly impossible. Before that I had been a style editor, writing and editing and full of creativity. But the darkness took away my words and to write was to climb a mountain too high. I could no longer work. I could barely get dressed. I moved lethargically from my bed to the loveseat, if I had even made it to my bed the night before. Some nights I did not abandon my post in the living room.

I moved in with my parents following my suicide attempt. I stayed with them for two years. I was relieved of my need to pay rent. I no longer had to buy food. Slowly my bank account wasted away. I couldn't pay my car payment any longer. I couldn't pay my phone bill. My parents took over. They did not keep a tally of money spent with the expectation of ever being repaid. There was no interest. They didn't want me to worry. They wanted only for me to get better.

In addition to my regular bills I was under a heavy financial burden already. I owed the IRS seven thousand dollars. It was a burden I had been carrying for months. My job in California was going to allow me to pay it. Make money, send money. But I had to resign when I lost my mind. There was no money. Then my grandmother stepped in and offered to pay the IRS for me. At first I was too proud to accept her help. But the days swept by and the deadline loomed. In the end there was nothing left to do but call her. Crying, I told her I needed her help. The weight was lifted and I was relieved and thankful.

At the free mental health center where I saw a psychiatrist and attended weekly bipolar support group meetings in Oklahoma I was assigned a triage specialist assistant, Eve. She suggested that I try to attain Social Security Disability. She handed me a phone number for the Social Security office. Mrs. Cameron at the office set a time for my interview. With all the medication I was taking I was in a perpetual fog so Eve offered to go with me to my interview. When I applied for Social Security Disability in May, seven months since leaving California, I had an empty bank account. My parents were still keeping me afloat.

The day of the meeting Eve and I took one of the mental health center's white cars and drove downtown. After a short wait we were led back to a small tan cubicle. The walls matched the carpet and everything was a shade of neutral, including Mrs. Cameron, who was a plump woman in her midforties with graying hair and round glasses. She didn't smile. She didn't make niceties. She immediately started in with her questions. What was my disability? When did I last work? How much money did I have in my bank account? How much money did I have on my person? Was I currently receiving any money from anyone? What were my expenses? Eve helped when she could, answering some questions for me, leaving others hanging in the air for me to catch and throw back. After half an hour, we were done. I left exhausted, with the knowledge that it could take months before I heard back as to whether or not I was approved.

In July I received a phone call from Mrs. Cameron. She told me that I had been approved for Social Security Disability. I would receive a deposit of $1,000 in my account on the third of every month. When I hung up I lay out on the floor of my cousin's room, where I was staying for the week. I felt myself sink into the ground and the earth began to cover me up. I called my mother and began to cry.

"So, I just found out that I will be getting disability," I said. "I feel like crap."

"This should be a good thing, Elaina," she said. "You can pay your bills now."

"I know, but I feel so low. It is like confirmation—'Yes, you are sick,'" I said. "I mean, the government has to help me."

"Honey, don't look at it that way. It doesn't mean it is forever, just 'til you get better. Try to see it that way," she said. "This is just for now."

We said our goodbyes and I hung up and lay there on the beige carpet, feeling the weight of my body on the floor. I felt like I was in a grave, like I was down so deep I would never get out.

The next month I took over my car payment and my phone bill. I paid my health insurance. I became an adult again. My bank account never grew, but it was enough to get by. I was receiving a quarter of what I was supposed to make in California but I was thankful for it, for every penny I was given.

Bipolar disorder is treated with medication and therapy. Medication is an important part of wellness and stability. I had to be vigilant. I had to take my medication every day. In Oklahoma at the mental health clinic, I received my medicine for free. I didn't have to pay for the half a dozen pills I took every day.

My job in California, though brief, allowed me health insurance. I was considered an employee, even though I had only been with the company for a week the first time I was hospitalized, so my insurance picked up some of the bill. The ambulance ride to the hospital and then from the first hospital to another with a psych ward cost nearly a thousand dollars. My hospital bill for the intensive care unit and the psych ward was many times that. My parents helped me out, putting their money with mine.

Following my resignation from the job, I continued my health insurance, paying a large but necessary premium. A third of the money I received through Social Security went to my health insurance.

When I was hospitalized for the second time in Lumberton, North Carolina, my insurance covered some of the bill. My seven-day stay cost me in the thousands of dollars. I could not afford it. I called the hospital and found out there was a plan to pay the balance over the next year interest free. I took them up on their offer and every month I submitted my payment.

I could extend my health insurance three years after I quit my job in California. That time came to an end just as I started graduate school. Before enrolling in the school's health insurance plan I called the company to ask whether bipolar disorder was covered. After much back and forth I was assured that it was.

I was with the plan for a couple of months when I went to the pharmacy to pick up my monthly prescriptions. I balked when the pharmacist told me that my medications were five hundred dollars. I had been paying about one hundred dollars for my pre-scriptions and didn't understand the sudden jump in price. I left my medicine there and called my insurance company the following day. I found out that there was a thousand-dollar cap on pre-scription drugs under the plan. With just one of my medications costing more than half of that a month, I had exceeded what the company would pay. I felt defeated.

Later that afternoon I called my sister-in-law, who worked for a nonprofit that supplied the needy with medication in her county. She told me to contact the drug manufacturers and see if they had programs for people who could not afford their med-ications. I found out the companies did offer assistance and, with the help of my psychiatrist, filled out applications. About a month later packages from both companies showed up, offer-ing three months of medicine and the option to refill three more times for the year at no cost.

After one semester, I left graduate school. I moved in with my boyfriend in Virginia and began to work on this book. I was without health insurance and paid for every minute I saw my psychiatrist. I put therapy on hold because I could not afford it.

When I was taken to the emergency room following my second overdose of Xanax, I didn't have insurance. I acquired charges for the day and night I was there and hundreds of dollars for the ambulance. When the bill for nearly two thousand dollars came for me, I worried. I contacted the hospital and applied for financial assistance. Three months later I got a response. They excused my costs—all but the ambulance.

At the Recovery Center, where I was taken for nine days fol-lowing my emergency room visit, I told the nurse the morning after I arrived that I could not afford to be there. She told me that it wouldn't cost me anything. Patients were not charged. While I was there my only worry was when I would get out, not how much it would cost me.

You must wait eighteen months after first receiving Social Security Disability before you are eligible for Medicare. In Jan-uary 2011, some information about Medicare came for me in the mail. There were booklets and websites and I was confused. I was college educated but it was like a foreign language I had never learned. I called a local senior services center and made an appointment to go over plans and forms and all that went along with the process. I was twenty-nine.

Ms. Clark was patient and searched eligible Medicare insurance plans with me to find the right one. I needed one that included mental health coverage and assisted during hospitalizations. I had no plan to be hospitalized, but gauging my past I knew that it was likely I would have to go into a psych ward again. She also told me about a program called Extra Help, in which Social Security helps a person pay for prescription medicine if their income is below a certain amount. I qualified and she helped me fill out those forms as well. By April I was on a Medicare health insurance plan.

Money was tight, so I had to forgo therapy. For more than a year I went without it. It came down to survival. Did I want to pay my car insurance or did I want to talk to someone for an hour a week?

Three years after my California suicide attempt I got a part-time job. I found something relatively easy—working retail at a fashion clothing store. I was overqualified and underpaid but it was a job and I was thankful for it. I needed the money and I found a purpose. There was a reason to get up early in the morning. There was a reason to leave the house. I adapted to the crazy schedule—some mornings up at four, some nights not leaving the shop until midnight. And in this menial job a hope began to grow. I wondered if maybe one day I might work full-time again. Maybe I would be an editor again. Maybe I would manage other people. Maybe all was not lost. In the back of my mind nibbled doubt. What would happen when I lost my mind again? It was a matter of time. But I quieted the voice.

A few months after I started work at my part-time job, I found a therapist and a new psychiatrist with offices just a few minutes away. Every time I visited them I paid them a co-pay of forty dollars. Some months it was tough. Sometimes after paying for my appointment at the end of the month, I had ten dollars left in my account.

I didn't have the money I used to. I was never rich (editorial work doesn't pay that well), but I always had enough. I could go out. I could eat out as often as I liked. I could go shopping. I could buy a round at the bar. I didn't have to worry about having enough for bills or food. But thirty dollars an hour full time versus eight dollars an hour part time, even with a thousand in disability, well, there really wasn't a comparison.

Bipolar disorder steals from you—time, money, relationships, hope. But that doesn't mean it is gone forever. It is just gone for a while, until you are back on your feet, until your medication and therapy put the broken pieces of you back together.

Maybe you have to work a little harder to undo what has been done. I have large, gaping holes in my resume. I have a non-existent bank account, but I know I will never go hungry, that I will always have a place to stay, because I am loved. Maybe you have to earn back what you can.

CHAPTER 20

Blog post

I'm feeling better today, not best, but better. I straightened my hair, put on a bright blue scarf. The kiddos are coming over today and I hope I have the needed energy for them. If not Elaina J. will have to take a time out up in her room. We'll probably go to IHOP with my boyfriend. They'll color on the activity mats and I'll order a veggie omelet. There will be laughter and coffee and maybe that's what I need. Maybe I need a bunch of little kids telling me knock-knock jokes. I don't know. But I can tell you it's sunshiny outside and it's filtering through the open blinds into this yellow room, creating a kind of glow. I can tell you I put on colorful argyle socks that go up to my knees and they are hidden under my jeans and that makes me smile. And smiling is winning the battle, even if it is a short-lived victory. I can't be well, but I can be better.

Better

My feet are furry.

Near the bone of my right ankle is a tuft of chocolate brown fur. I reach down and stroke it, feeling the soft hairs on my fingertips. I call out to my boyfriend and he comes into the room and sits next to me on my antique couch as I clutch the wooden arm. I look at him and see that his hands are made of sawdust. I don't know what is holding them together. There is a box full of nail polish sitting on the coffee table where I rest my feet. The blue shoebox is sparkling, diamonds winking at me. I watch as everything on the table begins to vibrate, dancing to some unheard song.

"What are you doing?" he asks.

"Nothing," I tell him, gazing again at his sawdust hands.

I look down at my own hands in my lap. They are covered in small dots like tapioca. Everything is becoming coated in the dots, like a foreign moss. Minutes go by.

"What are you doing, Elaina?" my boyfriend asks again.

"There is fur on my feet."

"What fur?"

"Here," I say as I pull at it. "I don't know how it got there."

"Elaina, there is no fur on your feet."

I consider this. "I think I might be hallucinating."

"Okay," he says. "What should we do?"

"Stay with me. I'm scared."

There is a grid in the air. I can see the currents of my breath as I exhale. I move my hands and watch the grid stretch and grow like something from high school geometry class. Jeremy watches me and when I look up at him I see confusion and concern on his face. The grid scares me. The dots scare me. His hands scare me.

The night before the hallucinations start I don't sleep. I don't know why I don't stay in bed with my boyfriend, why I don't sleep safely by his side. But as he sleeps I get up and make my way into my room, the one that houses all of my own things—my place in his house, and turn on the television. I stay up watching cable T.V. and movies, never tiring. It is the beginning of mania but I don't catch it, I don't see it for what it is.

In the morning my boyfriend has to go into work for a few hours. He kisses me goodbye and I melt further into the couch. When he comes home we chat and snuggle and things seem okay. A few hours later he is lying on the tan suede couch downstairs taking a nap. I put on a sexy negligee—all pink and black, breasts overflowing. I come downstairs and I get on top of him, straddling him beneath me. I start to kiss his full lips and reach my hand between his legs, pulling down the zipper. We make love. Me on top, then him. I don't climax. I can't when I am manic. It's all give and no take.

We change our clothes—he into his Navy uniform, me into a dress. He holds the door for me like a gentleman as I climb into his black pickup truck. On the way to the base he blasts his iPod and sings along. I feel the warmth of his fingers wrapped up with mine and lift his hand to my lips to kiss it. I am drowsy by the time we get to NAS Oceana, where he is an instructor, and I stay in the truck, dozing in and out of consciousness, while he goes in to muster the students he teaches.

When they are done, he comes and gets me and takes me into his building, shows me the classroom in which he teaches. I see electronic equipment meant for jets. I flip switches, turn knobs. He shows me his office and I sit in his chair and twirl in it like a small child, around and around. I don't remember what I saw. I don't remember the color of the floor or the objects on the wall. Nothing. It is all gone.

He tells me we stopped at a mini-mart for a snack. I got an energy drink and some Corn Nuts. I admire their strength, their resistance against my teeth. Then we went to the bowling alley to find out if they had any leagues starting and to get some information on the prices of the games and shoe rentals. I know this because I found a flyer in my purse days later. Afterward, we went shopping at the commissary. I came prepared with a list and it seems like we stuck to it. I can't tell you what the commissary looked like inside, how the aisles were laid out, where the meat counter was. When I go in again it will be for the first time.

When I am manic my mind leaves my body. I have conversations I forget. I am sexual and do things with my body I don't remember. I go places, do things, exist without consciousness. I have no memory of what I have done or why. Time eludes me. There is no anchor, nothing to hold me down. It is scary living this way, never knowing when I may float away.

It is after we get home that the hallucinations start. Fur. Sawdust. Grids in the air. It is imagined but real, so real I can touch it. I call my mom.

"What's the matter?" she asks immediately, hearing something in my voice that only mothers can hear.

"I'm hallucinating," I say as calmly as possible.

"Where's Jeremy?"

"He's here. Downstairs. I'm okay, Mom. It's just scaring me a little bit."

"Well, he needs to keep an eye on you. Call Dr. Jones and see what he says."

"Let's just see how it goes," I say.

"Elaina, if you are hallucinating maybe there is something he can tell you to do."

"Okay. Listen, I am going to go. I don't really feel up for talking. I just wanted to keep you in the loop. Don't worry too much. I am safe."

"Of course I am going to worry. I am your mother. Just call me any time if you need to. Any time, Elaina."

"I will," I say. "I love you."

"I love you, too."

I don't call my doctor. It is the weekend and I hate to disturb him by calling his emergency number. Instead I will stare at the grid in the air—pushing it, feeling its weight.

I sleep that night. Soundly. Safely. Then, in the morning, I wake up my boyfriend with a blowjob. I take him in my mouth and feel his warm skin with my tongue. His groan is a sound reserved just for this. I lift my head and make a trail of kisses up his soft stomach and firm chest to his neck. I feel the warmth of his body against my large breasts and gasp as he enters me.

He is working from afternoon to late evening and leaves at twelve-thirty. I want him to stay, to hold my hand. I don't get out of my pajamas all day, unable to summon the strength to shower, let alone change my clothes. I sit on my couch and watch reality television, episode after episode of "The Hills." I watch some movies. I watch the clock. When he comes home at ten-thirty I am asleep on the couch and so exhausted I stay there all night.

The next day is more of the same. I am low. Low enough that it feels like the ground can't hold me up. I manage a shower and a clean pair of underwear. I talk to my mom and she tells me to come home. She wants to keep me safe, to ward off the snakes at my feet.

And then suddenly I am sitting on the bathroom floor with an X-Acto blade. I stare at my left wrist, at its tangle of scars like dried-up rivers. I take the point and push it into the skin, piercing it. I cut a two-inch line away from my fingertips towards my elbow. I retrace the line again and again, making the cut deeper with each sweep. When I am done I hold a wad of toilet paper on it and sit there on the tiles with my left foot on the navy bath mat. When the bleeding lessens, I pull an extra large bandage from a box under the sink that I keep for moments like these.

My boyfriend comes home and I show him the bandage and tell him what I've done. His face seems angry but his voice is soft, soothing.

"Why did you do that, babe?" he asks.

"I don't know." And I don't. One minute I was on the couch, the next minute I had a blade in my hand. How the two are connected is lost to me.

"You can't do that. You can't cut yourself," he says. "Promise me you won't."

"I'll try," is all I can muster.

A few hours later I am back in the bathroom. My nightgown is short and it is only my panties that separates me from the floor. I pick a new blade from the pack of five. I want to be sanitary. I don't want an infection, just a hole. I tear off the extra large bandage, the biggest size I could buy, slowly so it doesn't hurt. I don't want it to hurt. I take the blade and go over the cut again, this time deeper. I feel it tug inside as I pull it through flesh. I do it again and again until I can't trace the cut because there is too much blood. I put a paper towel around it but the bleeding doesn't stop. I am alarmed and I call out to my boyfriend. He comes into the bathroom and asks me what I've done. I tell him it won't stop bleeding. We rinse it out and there is a clot of blood stuck to one side of the cut. He wraps my wrist in a paper towel but it soaks through. He goes to the kitchen and comes back with a crimson dishtowel, the color of my blood. He wraps my wrist in paper towels and then in the kitchen towel and tells me to hold it tight. I hold onto it for what feels like a long time. Then I check it and it is no longer a river but a creek. I put another bandage on it.

As we lay down to go to bed I tell my boyfriend he must stay awake because I am afraid of what I might do in the night, afraid of the death snaking up my wrist. He promises and I fall asleep as the bandage becomes soaked with blood.

We oversleep the next morning. We are supposed to meet my mom halfway between her house and mine so I can stay with my parents for a while. I hurry to gather my things, feed the dogs and let them out and back in again, and grab my laptop. As we pass from Virginia into North Carolina I call my psychiatrist and make an appointment for the following afternoon. Jeremy and I meet my mom at Starbucks and he passes me and my dog off.

When we get to my parents' house I go up to the guest bathroom and before I can get my shorts off I pee on myself. My shorts are wet, my underwear is wet, the floor is wet. I clean myself up, embarrassed, and put on my pajamas at five o'clock in the afternoon before taking my soiled clothes down to the washing machine. The night is a blur. I get my parents to take me to the store, where I buy a box of bandages. I pick up a pack of X-Acto blades and slide them into the bandage box. But even though part of my mind has left me, I know I can't shoplift so I pull them back out. Then I pick out some cardstock with the excuse of making a card for my friend's birthday. I need the X-Acto blades to cut the cardstock. We check out and somehow the bandages go unnoticed. Or perhaps they have already seen the one on my wrist and are not saying anything about it. Not yet.

That night I as I lay in bed my mom opens the door and asks if I have been cutting again. I tell her no and she says there is blood on the bathroom floor, so I admit to it. The next day she demands I give her the blades but I keep a knife wrapped in a paper towel under the sink. Just in case.

Thursday afternoon I am sitting in my psychiatrist's office.

"What's been going on, Elaina?" he asks.

"I didn't sleep on Saturday night and on Sunday I had hallucinations. Monday and Tuesday I couldn't get off the couch and then Tuesday night I cut myself."

I pull the Band-Aid away and reveal the ugly gash I've been working on.

"Oh, Elaina! You need stitches for that. Why did you do that?"

"I don't know. I can't explain it. I was sitting on my couch one minute and the next minute I was sitting on the bathroom floor cutting myself," I say. "I don't have to go to the hospital, do I?"

"Don't you think you should be there? Look what you are doing."

"But I can stay with my parents. My mom is here with me. I really don't want to go to another hospital."

"I am glad your mom is here. I am going to give you a shot of Geodone. You won't be able to drive afterwards so she will have to drive you."

"What's going on with me?" I need to know.

"You are going through a mixed episode, which means you are experiencing both the symptoms of mania and depression. The Geodone should help level things off. I am going to write a prescription and have you come back in on Monday for another one," he says. "Meanwhile stop taking the Cymbalta and let's add some Lithium. Why don't you go get your mother?"

I go out into the waiting room and call my mother, who is chatting with another patient and quilting. She gathers her things and follows me into Dr. Jones's office. I introduce the two.

"What about the stitches?" I ask.

"You need to go to an urgent care facility and get that taken care of," he says.

"But what if they want to send me to the hospital?"

"Tell them I sent you and that your mother is with you. If they have any questions they can call me."

He finishes mixing the Geodone powder with distilled water and pulls the liquid into a syringe. "Now pull down your pants. I need your right hip."

I do as he says and feel the prick of the needle.

I thank him and leave his office and go to the receptionist's window and make an appointment for the following week. I am not sure if it is the shot or the mania but the world is becoming even more off kilter. I follow my mom out into the summer sun.

We are unfamiliar with the urgent care facilities in the area, a forty-five minute drive from my parents' home, but are near the city hospital, so we drive around until we spot a clinic and stop. I stagger inside to ask if they take my insurance and can treat me. They say no, so it's back into the hot car, where my mother calls my sister-in-law, who grew up here in Fayetteville, North Carolina. She tells us of a place down the street a few blocks down, so we go there and they tell me that they do accept my insurance. They hand me a clipboard of forms to fill out and I ask my mother to help me because I am having trouble making sense of the questions and having even more trouble remembering the answers about doctors and hospitalizations and medication. I just want to go home. I just want to close my eyes and forget about stitches and Geodone shots and the way the world is swaying.

A short, blonde young woman calls my name and leads me and my mother back to an antiseptic room. I tell her what I've done and peel off the bandage.

"You do need stitches, but unfortunately it is too late for that. There is a window of time in which you can get stitches and you have exceeded that," she tells me. "What we can do is tape it up and let it grow back together."

She pulls open a drawer and gathers her supplies.

"Are you going to clean it out first?" I ask her

"Yes," she says and smiles up at me. "Clean it, then get it put back together."

She pours some clear liquid over and through it. It feels cool and I think of swimming in Barton Springs, a natural spring in Austin. I remember how I wore a waterproof bandage on my cut wrist back then but I could still feel the caress of the water on my delicate skin. She dabs at my wrist carefully, drying it with a noticeable sensitivity. Then she grabs some tape. She holds the gash together, letting it rise slightly as it touches. It takes seven pieces of tape to close it. Next, she pulls out some soft white gauze and wraps my wrist up in it before taping it shut.

"Now, you need to keep this dry for the next four days. You are going to leave the tape on until it falls off on its own. I am going to give you a prescription for an antibiotic," she says. "Take it all."

And with that I am out the door and into the car and on my way home, stopping first at the pharmacy to fill the prescriptions for Lithium and the antibiotic. I am there but gone. My mind has left me. A pharmacy tech calls out my name and I sign a sheet of paper relieving them of the responsibility of any bad reaction to the drugs. Finally, we are home and I make my way up the wooden stairway, a mountain, and find the bed in the guest bedroom. I crawl up onto it, face first. Then, I sleep.

I don't know if the Geodone is helping. I feel so low. I don't wash my face or get out of my pajamas the next day. It is all I can do to brush my teeth. I sit with my parents in the morning on the porch before the day heats up. I listen, but offer nothing to the conversation. When it is time for breakfast I eat because there is nothing else to do but eat. It is so much work—lifting my spoon, chewing my granola, trying not to cry. Then I feed my dog. No matter how I feel, no matter what little I am able to do, I take care of my dog.

After breakfast I climb back up the stairway and crawl back into bed, where I lay and look through the white eyelet curtains out the window. I lie here for hours, only getting up to go the bathroom or let the dog out. My mother checks on me, opening the door, asking if I want to watch a movie or go for a walk. But I don't. I want to die and the closest I can come to this is lying here as though I am dead.

I wake up wet. I have peed in my sleep. When I am manic I lose control—of myself, of my bladder. I go to the bathroom at three in the morning and wash off. I put on a clean nightgown. I go back to the mattress and attack it with a towel. When I have done all I can I lay a clean, dry towel down and crawl back into bed. When I wake in the morning there is a grass green towel beneath me, a reminder that it wasn't a bad dream.

On Monday I go back in to see Dr. Jones. I leave the waiting room to wash my hands in the bathroom. I stand at the sink and wash them twenty-five times. Pump the soap twice. Lather. Rinse. Repeat. I want to stand there for hours, forever. Pump-lather-rinse-repeat. Pump-lather-rinse-repeat. When I return to the waiting room my mom tells me that the doctor has called me. I knock on his door and enter his office when he replies.

"How are you doing, Elaina?" he says. "Are you noticing any improvement?"

"I was really depressed last week but seem to be doing a little bit better yesterday and today." Somehow I smile. "I don't want to die today so that's good."

"Well, these shots should help. I want you to come back in on Wednesday and Thursday to get one again. Okay?"

"Okay."

"Is your mom with you to drive you again?"

"Yes. She is out in the waiting room," and I feel the prick of the needle as it enters my skin.

I take the series of shots and am so tired afterward that I have to take a nap when I get back to my parents' house each afternoon. The mania subsides but the depression cycles still. One day I am up for a walk in the morning with my dad and the next I spend lying on my bed imagining my funeral. I decide my sister will do my makeup for the viewing. She does her own so beautifully and I want to look like myself, not some doll. I wonder if they let a relative do the makeup, if they leave them alone with the corpse.

A week later I am well enough to go with my mother for a visit to my grandmother's house. We drive two hours, stopping at a roadside stand to buy fresh peaches and eat a cone of homemade ice cream. The cold is refreshing on my tongue and the waffle cone is crisp and sweet. We arrive at my grandmother's house, where my two younger cousins are playing. They tell me about their favorite movie and show me their toy cars. We sit on the couch and take photos together. My grandmother talks and talks as her little dogs bark. She is ravenous for adult company.

A few hours later my uncle arrives to pick up the boys. We visit and he tells me about his advertising sales work, how he won rookie of the year at the job. Shortly after, my aunt arrives and sits on the floor, flipping through a magazine and listening to the conversation. But it is all too much for me. The family, the noise, the attention. I go to the bathroom and take a few Klonopin pills prescribed for my anxiety. Then a few more. My cousins leave with my aunt and uncle. My mom and grandmother leave the kitchen to go in the backyard with her dogs and I quickly search the cabinets for some alcohol. I haven't had a drink in three months, not since my stay at the Recovery Center, but suddenly can't live another moment without one. I find an amber bottle of apricot brandy and take a swig. It will have to do.

I call my boyfriend. He doesn't answer so I text him: Call me. Crisis. When he calls me ten minutes later I tell him I've taken some pills and about the brandy. He sounds angry at me and my voice becomes little.

"I'm not angry, I'm frustrated. Why are you taking so many pills?"

"Because I'm stressed out. All the people," I say. "It's just too much."

"Well, don't take any more. Give them to your mom. Just stop, Elaina."

We get off the phone and I feel more alone than I had before talking to him. I don't know how I am going to get through the night. I take another three pills. By now I've taken ten of my one milligram dose. I feel the same.

When I wake up in the morning I am sleepy and my voice is slightly slurred. I stumble to the bathroom and wash my face, hoping the cold water will snap me out of the fog. I sit at the kitchen table and eat apple fritters and drink warm coffee with cream. My mother asks me if I am okay and I tell her I am really tired.

My mom's cell phone rings. It is my little sister. My mom talks to her for a few minutes before handing the phone to me.

"Hi," she says. "I have something I want to tell you." I can hear excitement in her voice.

"What?" I ask, but already know. I love her but I am not ready to hear it. Not yet. Not now.

"I'm engaged!" she squeals.

Something in my throat catches as I try to speak. "Congratulations! I am so happy for you."

I give the phone to my grandmother and go to the bathroom, allowing myself a momentary breakdown. I cry because my life has become a series of breakdowns, of mania and depression, and it is far from the way it once was. My sister's life is moving forward—career, sunny San Diego, engagement—and mine keeps taking steps backward. I cry because it doesn't seem fair.

Back at my parents' house that evening I am jonesing for a cigarette. It's a sign of my mania, I've recently figured out. I told my doctor about it and he explained that smoking cigarettes allows your brain to communicate with itself. When you are manic this ability is limited. I tell my parents I am going for a walk and walk a mile to the drugstore.

"Which of these cigarettes is most like American Spirit?" I ask the clerk.

"I don't know," she says in a condescending tone. "I've never smoked a cigarette."

"Fine. I'll take the Pall Malls," I say choosing a cheap brand.

"In the red box?"

"I don't know. Sure."

We make the transaction and I walk out of the store, only then remembering that I need a lighter. I go back in and buy a lighter from another clerk, this one friendlier. I walk until I am between bushes and a creek and light up like I am a fourteen-year-old hiding from my parents. I am thirty years old and am, in fact, hiding from my parents. When my mother found out I had been smoking in California she was disappointed. This must be a secret, just one of the many. I fill my lungs with smoke and feel myself calm—not entirely, but some.

When I return home from my walk my parents ask me if I want to go with them to watch the fireworks. It is the Fourth of July. I tell them no, that I don't want to go anywhere but that they should go without me. My mom is worried about leaving me alone but I shoo them off. When they are gone I call my doctor's number and write down the emergency number given on the recording. I dial it and an answering service operator's voice fills the line, I tell her that I need Dr. Jones to call me and give her my phone number. I hop in the shower and quickly wash off the sweat from my walk. I'm out and in my pajamas when he calls me back.

"What's going on?" he asks.

"I think I am beginning to get manic again. I took a lot of pills last night and tried to drink. And my sister got engaged. Then today I bought some cigarettes—and you know I don't smoke. I am just starting to feel a little nutty."

"Okay. I want you to up your dose of Saphris by one pill for a couple of days. See if that helps, if not, call me."

We get off the phone and I flop on the bed. There is nothing to save me. The anxiety pills won't save me. The cigarettes won't save me. I can't walk far enough for salvation. For now, I must endure.

I take the extra Saphris pill each morning for the next few days and am noticeably groggy. My parents tell me they can hear it in my speech. But it keeps me from mania and for that I am thankful. I start to feel better as the days go by. Not good, but better. And sometimes that is all I can ask for—better.

CHAPTER 21

Blog post

"It's okay to be okay."

That is what my therapist told me. Here we are, July 2012, and I haven't been hospitalized since March 2011. And I am waiting for the wildfire. You see, I get nervous when things start going too well. Because if anything, I have proven unpredictable.

"It's okay to be okay." It's okay to sit back and relax a little. It's okay to not worry about what is going to happen when the shit hits the fan. It's okay to quit thinking "when" and imagine "if." And if it is okay to be okay, and it is okay to be sick, it is okay to just be.

I'm standing here with my bucket of water and I'm waiting for the fire but it turns out it is going to rain. After all.

My therapist is smart and I trust her. I have thought about what she has said. I've let it marinate. And I like it. I want to stop waiting for the fire. I want to wake up and write and live and love and laugh and cry and be okay!

I don't want to live waiting for my next hospital visit, imagining the bad coffee and cold toast. The flip side of being sick is being well. And I am well. Let's stop and celebrate that! Stop wishing it away in preparation!

So I am going to actively push my fear aside and breathe. I am going to savor today and yesterday. Tomorrow will come. Give it time.

You Talk, I'll Listen

"Hi, Elaina. It's Arianna."

I hadn't heard from my therapist since I had returned home from California to Oklahoma following my suicide attempt and here she was on my cell phone inside Blockbuster. I walked outside and sat down on the curb, stretching my green sneakers out in front of me on the black asphalt of the parking lot.

"Hi, how are you?" I said.

"I'm fine. Do you remember talking to me when you were in the hospital?"

I didn't.

"Vaguely."

"I am very sorry for what happened to you, Elaina," she paused. I listened. "I can no longer be your therapist."

The last time I had felt this way was when Blair told me he wasn't interested in taking our relationship to the next level over a dinner he cooked for me at his apartment in Austin. It kind of felt like I had been hit in the stomach.

"What?"

"I can't provide you with the support you need. You need to find a new therapist there in Oklahoma. We will no longer be in contact."

I swallowed.

"Elaina?"

"Yes?"

"This is for your safety. I will be sending you something in writing."

"Okay," I said.

"Take care, Elaina. Goodbye."

The line went silent and I pulled the phone from my ear. I stared at the small screen, then focused on an old grey Dodge pickup truck in the space next to my feet. How could Arianna leave me? Weren't therapists supposed to help you? Didn't she care what happened to me?

I blinked back tears and stood. I pulled the elastic out of my hair and massaged my head before pulling my curls back up into a ponytail. I turned around, took a deep breath, and walked back into Blockbuster.

Arianna had been my therapist for over a year. I originally saw her at the University of Texas' counseling center. I went to the UT center because I learned that they provided services to patients in Austin on a sliding scale, and because I didn't have health insurance at my magazine job, that was a necessity. When Arianna went off to start her own practice I followed her. She was beautiful, with glossy black hair and big blue eyes. It seemed as though she was perpetually in a pencil skirt and heels and as someone who cared about fashion, I cared about this. Her voice was soft and her questions gentle. I was never comfortable in therapy but I was comfortable enough to open up to her. I talked about Ashton and the harassment. I explained my anxiety to her, how I was afraid to go to the grocery store, how I couldn't make it down to the frozen foods in the back of the store before fleeing. I cried to her when my high school sweetheart got engaged. We talked about my work and about my stress.

When I left Austin to move to Oklahoma for a couple of months, I was scared to leave Arianna. She was the keeper of my secrets. She was my guide. We worked out a plan to have phone sessions. After all, we were just talking and what was the difference if she could see my face or not? Once a week I would settle into the big leather chair in my dad's home office and dial her number. We would talk for fifty minutes and then we were done until the following week. It wasn't as good as sitting on her comfy couch, but it worked.

Then I went to California.

Then I tried to kill myself.

I don't blame Arianna for ending our professional relationship. I believe she was right. She couldn't help me in the way I needed to be helped at the time. But it sure felt like a breakup, like I was being dumped by someone who knew me so well but decided they no longer wanted me.

My next therapist was Andrea. She had a Ph.D. I thought this would make her a good match, like holding a certain level of degree would somehow save me. In her office in Norman, Oklahoma, were children's toys because she also treated kids. When I spoke to her I looked at the bright reds and deep blues of these toys and wondered who played with them. I wondered if I would ever play again.

I was still delicate when I went to Andrea. I had only recently been glued back together. The glue was still tacky. I needed someone to give me my confidence back. I needed someone who could assure me that I wouldn't lose my mind again, to tell me that it wasn't still lost. She couldn't do that, and the truth is that no one could have, but I faulted her for that, for not being who I wanted her to be. I saw Andrea for six months and in that time never grew close to her. Our relationship was nothing like the one I had with Arianna. I never felt like Andrea understood what I was saying, as though we needed a translator to work out our conversations.

Eventually I left Andrea for Luanne. I met Luanne at the mental health clinic where I received psychiatric care in Norman, Oklahoma. She was the facilitator for my bipolar disorder support group. She was kind, compassionate, and smart. When her schedule allowed for an open spot for individual counseling, she took me on. What was great about Luanne was that she got it. She understood bipolar disorder in all its nuances. I would sit in her tiny office and she would grab her dry-erase marker and draw diagrams to depict feelings. Together we made lists of my personal challenges and then one by one addressed them. She, like me, was a problem solver. She didn't just ask how I was feeling; she tried to figure out how I could feel better.

The summer of 2009 I moved with my parents to North Carolina. My psychiatrist in Oklahoma advised me to seek treatment at Duke University because of its renowned psychology and neuroscience department. He told me it was worth the drive if I could be seen by the professionals at Duke.

I ended up in the hands of Melissa, a graduate student at Duke. At the time my obsessive compulsive rituals were insane. The stress of the move and new environment caused me anxiety. The anxiety then in turn caused my OCD to spike. Upon meeting Melissa I could not shake her hand, I was too afraid of her germs. Melissa meant well, really, she did. She had me fill out a "dialectical behavior therapy diary card." Each week, on the chart, among other things, I rated my urges to self-harm, suicidal urges, my hours of sleep, and my levels of mania, and I rated my feelings, including anger, sadness, joy, and fear. At our weekly scheduled appointment, she would look over the diary card to assess how I was doing. But being with Melissa made me feel like a school project. She was, in fact, still in school and had not yet been licensed. I didn't feel like she was capable of treating me and my severe symptoms.

Duke was about an hour and a half away from my parents, so once a week I made the three-hour round trip drive north and back. I gave it four months. I was also seeing a psychiatrist who was a Duke professor. But my care didn't seem to warrant the drive. In January, I looked for someone closer to home.

I fell in love with my next therapist. Dr. Hudson held a doctorate of psychology and a masters of divinity. Her approach to therapy had a spiritual side that I relished. I had always had strong faith in God and in therapy we could talk about Him, an important part of my life. I stayed with Dr. Hudson for another six months and reluctantly left her care when I moved to Wilmington to attend graduate school at the University of North Carolina Wilmington.

Up next was Sarah. She also held a Ph.D. My first impression of her was that she was too young. She appeared to be around my own age and I wasn't sure if she was qualified to be my therapist. I worried that she didn't have the experience with severe bipolar patients that I wanted her to have. I gave her a chance, though, and was pleasantly surprised. Talking to her was a lot like talking to a friend. She listened to what I had to say and offered advice and guidance.

I didn't stay in graduate school. It wasn't the right fit for me at the time. Taking a leave of absence meant moving from Wilmington, which meant leaving Sarah. My last appointment with her was just before Christmas and I was scared to be walking into an uncertain future in which I had no therapist to help me handle my stress or deal with my illness.

And then there was a lull. I moved to Virginia, in with my boyfriend, and though I had a psychiatrist, I did not seek out a therapist. I didn't have insurance for four months and that was my excuse at first—it was too expensive. I had never enjoyed therapy. I didn't like exposing myself the way I was expected to. And I was doing just fine, thank you very much. I didn't need therapy anymore. I was better.

Then I overdosed again on Xanax.

On purpose.

A month after I was released from the Recovery Center I qualified for Medicare. So I got myself insured and sought a therapist. It was challenging to find someone who would accept my insurance but I managed to get an appointment with Cathy.

I didn't like Cathy from the start. Her hair was frizzy and her clothes were ugly and as a former fashionista, it gave me the impression that she didn't care. And if she didn't care about herself, how in the world was she going to care about me? I handed her the forms I had filled out about my background and my hospitalizations and my many medications. She looked them over and asked me a few questions, which I reluctantly answered. Then I asked her about herself. I wanted quality care. She was a former army nurse who had only been counseling for two years. This, I deemed, was not enough time to be well-versed in mental illness. I wanted a professional with years under her belt. That was the first and last time I saw Cathy.

It was eight more months before I reached out for help again. After all, I had tried, hadn't I? I had tried to find a therapist, and when I had found one she wasn't good enough so why bother?

Plus, I didn't have to talk about myself to a stranger, which was an added bonus.

In January of 2012 I needed a new psychiatrist. I landed at a Christian mental health service. In order to be treated by a psychiatrist at the office I had to also receive counseling by someone in the office. For one session I saw Joy. She was little and pleasant and talked so fast I had trouble understanding her. But it turned out that she did not accept my insurance. There was a new therapist starting at the practice who happened to be Joy's sister. Instead of waiting another month and half to be seen by someone on a weekday I agreed to come in on a Saturday and see Maya.

I liked Maya right away. Her first impression was a good one. She was petite and fashionable, with highlighted hair. When she spoke to me she looked me in the eyes. When she asked a question she waited patiently for me to answer. She asked me to keep a journal of my feelings, especially those revolving around self-harm. During our session every other week she would look over the journal and ask questions. It was a good tool to see patterns and try to understand the reasons I acted the way I did. In a way, she was like Dr. Jones. As a Christian she freely peppered her conversations with talk of God.

"Lately I've been getting nervous. I haven't been in the hospital in over a year," I said.

"And you're waiting for the other shoe to drop?" Maya asked.

"Yeah, kind of. I mean, this is the longest I have gone since all this madness started. It seems that I can go just over a year and then the shit hits the fan and I end up back in the hospital," I said. "I'm just waiting for it to happen again."

"Elaina, it is okay to be okay. You don't have to wait for something bad to happen. If you have to go back in the hospital tomorrow, then we will deal with that, but you shouldn't expect it. You can choose to be happy now."

After our session I thought about what she had said and decided she was right. I could choose to be okay. I could choose to be happy. I was doing better, more stable. Would I have episodes again? Likely. But I didn't need to sit around waiting for them. I decided to quit thinking about "when" they would come but rather "if" they would come. If there was the possibility of being sick, then there was the possibility of being well. Ying. Yang. It was an active way of thinking. I had to quiet the voices that said, "It's coming. Just wait."

I decided to celebrate my life. I had nearly died a couple of times. I had been incapacitated. I had suffered. I had lost. But I was alive. I was well. I was ready to live.

CHAPTER 22

Blog post

My illness is a dark thing in the back of my mind. It does not come out and play. It stays safely in the recesses. There are puppies and babies. There is sun in the sky.

It's been six months since my last manic episode. Six months and I celebrate. The last time there were more doctors and medicines. There were wounds seen. There were wounds hidden beneath skin and lies and vanishing smiles. There was less hope and more just getting by.

It isn't easy, getting up each day not knowing. For me there is that nagging, that dark thing that lurks, waiting. I cannot trust in the sun, for it sets, and rarely are the stars bright enough.

I've got a life—a boyfriend, long chats with my mother, two dogs to take care of, a house to clean. I've got a life and it matters. I cannot be bothered with clouds.

I want so much. So much. So much more. It's been six months and in me has grown hope. What if it could always be this way? No more doctors. No more shade.

But the thing about this illness is that it sneaks up. It attacks without so much as a growl. One day you are at the beach, the next you are on a mountaintop in a storm.

I cannot count on tomorrow. I can't count on tonight. But I can stand up and say, "I was here. For today, I was here."

Sex

My sex life is often dictated by my illness. Sometimes I am hypersexual, other times I am asexual. It depends on a myriad of factors. Mania. Medication. Depression.

When I am manic, when my mind is reeling, my body becomes hypersensitive. A simple kiss on the neck and my nipples harden. A stoke of my forearm makes my heart beat faster. I don't want to kiss; I want to devour.

When I am manic, I become sexy. I wear revealing lingerie. I forget my panties. I whisper dirty words in my boyfriend's ear at our favorite restaurant. In mania, I love my full breasts and the curves of my hips; even the roundness of my stomach is enticing.

When I am manic I want sex. I crave it. I need it. Right now. In the bed. In the shower. On the couch. On the floor. I climb on top of my boyfriend, straddle him in a red negligee, lean down and bite his lip, put his hand on my ass. I tell him I want him because I do.

When I am manic there are problems. I cannot climax, no matter how turned on I am. It is impossible and elusive and frustrating. I want it so bad, that satisfaction, that buzz, that release. It leaves me wanting more. And more. And more.

Depression falls on me a lot more often than mania. When I am depressed I want to disappear. I don't want to have sex because to have sex I would have to exist. I don't want to "make love" because I don't deserve love. I don't deserve to be touched and kissed. I can't feel good because I have forgotten how.

When I am depressed the bed becomes a place to hide, not to play. My sexy nighties are left in dresser, on the back of the bathroom door. I wear baggy pajamas because I don't want him to see my body. I don't want to have a body. I don't believe him when he says I am sexy. The same body that I relish when I am manic becomes a body I despise when I am depressed.

It's there in the fine print, in the "side effects" information. Sexual dysfunction. I have taken antidepressants on and off for over a decade. Inevitably, those tiny pills find their way into my covers. My sex drive follows a road out of town. I am simply not interested.

On some drugs the desire hangs around but orgasms take a hike. During a recent stint on Zoloft, my orgasm went missing for six months. Having sex with my boyfriend was just frustrating, so I didn't really want to do it. I knew how it would end, and I wasn't interested in that particular result.

"You've got to talk to the doc about your meds," Jeremy says.

We are lying naked on our bed after sex. He tried to make me happy, to make me orgasm. I couldn't.

"I know. I will. It's just..." I sigh. "You don't understand how embarrassing it is. I mean, I respect him, but he isn't a warm man and talking to him about our sex life is not something I am looking forward to."

"Well, babe, I think we have a problem here."

"I know," I say. "I am the one who is suffering. I know we have a problem."

"Do you want me to talk to him?" I can tell he is smiling in the dark. "Shoot. I'll be like 'Doc! We have a serious problem! My baby needs to orgasm. Fix it!'"

I laugh and squeeze his hand. I know he loves me.

Later that week I sit in my Christian psychiatrist's office.

"So, Elaina, anything you want to tell me? Any new medications or problems?"

"Um, no new medications except for the ones you prescribe. But, I am having a problem," I say. "When I have sex I can't seem to orgasm."

"How long have you had this problem? Have you talked to your counselor about it?"

"Yeah, and she—we—think it probably is related to the

Zoloft because it has been going on about as long as I have been on it."

"Well, sexual dysfunction is a side effect of SSRIs. Would you like to try something else and see if maybe that helps?"

"Yeah. The Zoloft has really helped with the anxiety so I hate to change it but this really is a problem for my boyfriend and I."

"Have you told your boyfriend that it might be the medication?" Dr. Balzer says. "How does he feel about it?"

"He knows. He thinks it is probably the medication too. He suggested I talk to you."

"All right, well, let's try Prozac. Ever taken it before?"

"Nope."

"You shouldn't have any problems switching over from one SSRI to the other. If you do, give me a call. I want to see you back in a couple of weeks to see how things are going."

He finishes writing out my prescriptions for Lamictal, Saphris and now Prozac. He makes some notes in my file.

"Would you like me to say a prayer before you leave?" he asks.

"Sure."

We bow our heads.

"Heavenly Father, thank you for helping Elaina with her anxiety and keeping her symptoms minimal. Thank you for keeping her from becoming manic or depressed. Bless this medication to work quickly and that she might have fewer side effects. All thy glory to your name. Amen."

"Amen."

My sex drive also seems correlated to my weight, which is ever-fluctuating on my series of medications. When I am "fat" I don't feel sexy. I hide under the covers. I wait until it is dark to show my body to my boyfriend. I have a hard time believing him when he tells me I am hot. I didn't feel hot twenty pounds ago; how am I expected to feel attractive now?

And how does a woman with obsessive compulsive disorder and anxiety about germs have sex? How does she kiss her boyfriend? Hold his hand? There have been times I have asked my boyfriend to get out of bed and go wash his hands, not because they are visibly dirty, but because I worry about the germs that might be on them. I cannot stand the thought of him touching my body until I believe they are clean. When we are out I squeeze antibacterial gel onto his palms before we can lock our fingers together. Although I have OCD, there are things that are "safe." My boyfriend is safe. I think I would probably have a panic attack if a stranger spit on me, but I can kiss my boyfriend's full lips without fear. I think it has something to do with intimacy, with love.

Sex isn't as easy or straightforward as Cosmopolitan magazine would have me believe. It isn't a matter of lingerie and the position of the month. There are too many factors, factors uncontrollable because of my illness. I wish I could have all the desire of mania without any of the complications. I would be a sex goddess. But my sexual confidence comes at a price, so I wish for something stable. I want to feel sexy and still have an orgasm. I want to love myself enough to make love.

CHAPTER 23

Blog post

There are people who love me for me, for the way I say "bagel" or "Rolling Rock." They love the way I laugh or smile or cry. To them there is nothing to change, even the annoying things, those little things that can grate. I am not perfect, but to them I am perfect enough.

I've always been hard on myself. Never quite good enough. Winning never made me the victor. Second was always second best. I always wanted so much for myself, expected so much of myself. I always had to succeed, exceed. There was never any margin of error. Only the best.

And then I got sick and everything changed. I could no longer lead the race. I fell behind. Far behind. And I felt like a failure for not running fast enough, hard enough. And then there were hospitals and doctors and medicine and therapy. And then the only flag blowing in the wind was the white one. No checkers. No winner.

There are people who love me for me. The incurable beast. The way I sniff my glasses. They know how close I have come to the edge, how quickly it can all change. They answer my calls. They visit me when I am in the hospital. They know that today isn't just a day, it is another day. And for all accounts I shouldn't be having any more of them.

I am lucky to be loved, to be held close, to see and feel and know love. It didn't take my illness for me to feel love, but my ill-

ness held up a magnifying glass. It showed me that I was good enough—even at my worst. Today I am a bit gentler. I don't expect perfection. I know that to many I am good enough, and that, for me, becomes good enough.

I have not risen above all of this, but I can believe in the love that is given to me. I can know that when they say I am beautiful that to them, I am. I can rest in their embrace. I can close my eyes beneath their smile. Love heals.

Blood is Thicker than Water

Love is a powerful thing. It strips away the madness, the irrational, and the dark. It raises me up when I've fallen down. It is a ladder when I fly into the stars.

My mother has been my cheerleader, my babysitter, my cook, my nurse, my driver, my best friend. She has come to visit me often when I have been in the hospital, and when I moved out of North Carolina she offered to drive hours just to see me for ten minutes in the Recovery Center in Virginia Beach. She brought me cookies and books and my favorite pale pink roses. She brought me sweatpants and clean underwear. She was always there for the five-minute phone calls I was allowed each day, filling me in on life on the outside, giving me hope for something normal. She never spoke to me like I was an invalid. Her words were natural, as though we were sitting at the dining room table.

My mother sees the light when I am dark. She offers me unending hope that things will get better and makes me believe that I will survive. After I tried to kill myself she and my father flew out from Oklahoma to California on the earliest flight they could take. I was still unconscious in intensive care. My parents stayed out in California while I lived for five days in the psych ward of Mills-Peninsula Hospital. They came twice a day, every day, to visit me. When I was released, she, along with my father and my sister, packed up my apartment, the apartment I had moved into just a week before. She and I boarded a plane and headed back to Oklahoma while my father drove my blue Scion

1,600 miles. She made sure there was a wheelchair for me at the airport when I was too weak from medication to walk.

She found me clutching my cut wrist and took me to the hospital the second time I was admitted to a psych ward. Every day she arrived early for visiting hour and I watched her through the glass in the door that separated us. I was bored from the lack of stimulation in the ward and her conversations were like a jolt of electricity. They woke me up, made me feel alive.

After my diagnosis, before every therapist or psychiatric appointment she bought me a cup of coffee at the coffee shop. She knew it helped me to play with the cup, to find distraction in those uncomfortable meetings. She sat with me in the waiting rooms as time crawled by. She loved me unconditionally.

A couple months after I nearly died, my father took me to lunch. We went to a Texas-inspired steakhouse. We sat across from each other in a wood and leather booth cracking peanuts from tin buckets and tossing the shells on the floor. It was nice, just he and I. I was still delicate and wrapped up in tissue paper. He began to talk about his mother, someone I had never met. He chewed on a peanut. Then his eyes met mine.

"We are strong," he said. "The Martins are strong."

I saw tears sparkle in his eyes and knew what he meant. He wanted me to fight. He didn't understand my illness but he knew that it could take away the life he had given to me.

In December he bought me a puppy, something to give me purpose, a reason to get up every day. I named her Hope because that is what I needed. My father gave me a place to lie down every night and food to fill me up. He relieved me of some of my worries. My father took care of me when I couldn't take care of myself.

We never discussed my illness. It made him uncomfortable. His "little one" was sick and there was nothing he could do to make her better. He's done so much for me but tells me he feels like he should be able to do more. When I have to go into the hospital he feels helpless even knowing that it is the best place for me at that time. It isn't that my father loves me any less than my mother does; he just handles my illness differently.

"I'm glad your mother is here," said Dr. Jones.

"Me, too."

In June 2011, we sat in Dr. Jones's office on his blue couch while he talked to us about Geodone shots and mania and stitches. I looked at the pictures of his sons on his desk. Beautiful children. And he looked at us, mother and child. He agreed to let me go home with her instead of to the hospital. Instead of doctors and nurses, my mother was the one to patrol me while on suicide watch. She made my dinner and opened the door to my bedroom late at night. Checking. She carefully watched me, letting me think I was in charge when really, already, I was leaning on her.

When I was too much for my boyfriend, when he couldn't be with me all the time because of work and kids and life, my parents took me in. We watched romantic comedies and chatted on the back porch. I wasn't sick with them. I was resting. I was getting well.

Nearly four years after I almost killed myself, my mother told me she was glad to get me home back then, yet she worried because watching me became her responsibility. There were no doctors, no nurses watching me around the clock, checking on me every few hours during the night to be sure that I hadn't somehow found a way to die. She was scared that if she didn't watch closely enough I would try it again and that this time I would be successful. She would sit up at night, waiting for my meds to kick in so I'd fall asleep before she went to bed. She felt like it was all up to her to keep me safe.

She says she worries about me, especially when I go into the hospital. She worries that I have gone off my medications, or that they are no longer working. Her mind goes to all the horrific things that could have happened to put me into a tail-spin. She wonders if I have hurt myself again, that maybe this time is worse than the last. And then she thinks about whether or not she will get me back, or if instead, I will be changed. That I am feeling so depressed that I will try to kill myself again or that I am flying too high and could easily slip and fall and die—that is her constant worry.

My mother has done her best to understand. She has read books on my illness—Loving Someone with Bipolar Disorder, and The Bipolar Relationship. She's attended NAMI (National Alliance on Mental Illness) meetings, sitting with other family members of the sick-minded. Talking with my doctors has enlightened her to an extent. She knows what is possible and has experienced what has happened along with me.

When I went off to graduate school, I returned home to my parents' house over an hour away nearly every weekend. I would pack up my books and my dog and head to their home. I didn't want to be alone with my thoughts. I wanted to feel their love wrapped around me like the handmade quilt my mother sewed for me. I ate my mom's cooking and watched television in the living room with my dad. It helped me stay well. It helped to lighten the darkness.

Growing up, my sister and I were inseparable. I am older by three and a half years and she looked up to me. As adults we took trips together—Mexico, the Bahamas, the Caribbean—and there were few people I would rather spend my time with. When the madness set in my sister was there for me. She was the one who spent her 24th birthday alone by my bed in a California intensive care unit. She had to call my parents halfway across the country and tell them that their daughter had tried to kill herself. It's hard to forgive myself for putting her through that. It is a guilt I carry around. Every day I was in the hospital in California she came to visit me, never mind her demanding advertising job. She came. She brought me pictures of my family and friends, reminders that I was loved. Her best friend made me brownies. She smiled for me.

After I moved back to Oklahoma I called her often. During long distance phone calls, she listened from California as I cried into the phone, night after night.

My moods were dramatic. She says she felt like sometimes she was the big sister instead of the little one, sometimes she was the friend, sometimes the cheerleader, and sometimes the punching bag. She no longer knew what to expect when she picked up the phone, but her biggest fear was that the voice on the other end would be telling her I had taken my own life. She grew tired of always having to be there. It is exhausting always holding someone up.

She told me she didn't believe that I could not remember what had happened in California. She called me a liar for telling the doctors and my family and my friends that I had no recollection of the events that caused me to try to take my life. She said that in the intensive care unit of the hospital that I told her I had planned my suicide attempt and that I had been angry for failing. I didn't understand. When I woke up the day of the attempt, that week, that month, I had no intention of killing myself. The only way I could explain it was to borrow the words of my doctors and call it a psychotic break.

My moods were volatile and the slightest irritation could cause me to lash out. For a moment I had let my irritability get the better of me and because I thought she was acting selfishly I told her to stop acting like a bitch. For her, that was enough. She was tired of putting up with my shit, tired of the phone calls, tired of my bad decisions, tired of picking me up every time I fell. She walked out of my life on a warm April day, throwing my mistakes in my face. She didn't talk to me for months. She blocked my number on her phone. She sent emails that hurt me, but she sent them because she was hurt too. I loved her so much it broke my heart. Then one day she sent me flowers: I love you and think about you every day. I'm not upset with you in any way. One day I hope to be strong enough to be there for you again.

My illness had pushed her away. I wondered how much I could blame her. How much of me was enough? A couple more months went by and we began to speak again. It was awkward and cumbersome and we were never the same after that. Our relationship had shattered, and even after gluing it back together there were cracks.

My cousin, Kimberly, screamed and dropped the phone when she heard that I had tried to kill myself. She had been the last one to talk to me and everything had seemed okay—better than okay. I had been happy, excited, talking a mile a minute. We had planned our future. We would date, then marry grads of the nearby Stanford University. Kimberly would become a lawyer. We would always be together. How I could, hours later, try to end my life was beyond her comprehension. She called me while I was in the hospital. Her words were careful, stepping lightly around me. She didn't ask me why I had done what I did; instead she told me that I was loved.

When I returned to Oklahoma Kimberly hugged me tightly, so tightly that if I close my eyes I can feel her arms around me still. We spent days together, she and I. We would sit at Starbucks talking for hours. We had so much to say and when it was quiet, when our words came to a stop, we resonated. She taught me to laugh again. She made me feel important, trusting me with her secrets, asking me to be a part of her intimate wedding. On the first anniversary of my suicide attempt Kimberly sent me a gift halfway across the country in the mail. Not to remember what had happened, but to celebrate my life.

It was hard for my brother to imagine what I went through. I was his little sister. He had spent his life looking out for me. He felt like he was supposed to protect me. During my hospital stay the first time, he could barely speak to me on the phone. He, like everyone else, didn't understand what had happened. When I was hospitalized in North Carolina, the state where he also lived, he came to visit. I could tell he was uncomfortable, that he'd rather be anywhere else than in a psych ward visiting his sister, but he came anyway. It meant so much to me to see his face, to feel his love.

There were cards from my grandmother and my aunt, re-minders that I was special, and in them I found hope that every-thing would be okay. My aunt wrote to me: Hello, sweetheart. I pray every day that you are able to cope with the life that has been given to you. With your eloquence in writing perhaps God's plan was for you to educate people on the depths of your ill-ness and their reactions/lack of understanding of what you go through on a daily basis. Perhaps in your writing abilities you can educate them enough to help you...I really just want you to know how much you are loved by your family and friends. And how very proud I am of you and your abilities. Just always remember how much I love you.

Her words would stay with me after she died from pancreatic cancer less than a year after it was discovered. Encouragement handwritten on a small piece of paper.

I reconnected with members of my family that I hadn't spoken to in years. They listened to me and offered support. I became close to a cousin who dealt with his own mental illness. His attention deficit disorder nearly incapacitated him. For years he had struggled with a racing mind. In him, I found an ally. He understood what it was like to be sick and he understood our family and how the two were intertwined.

My family did not cure me. There is no cure for my madness. They have picked up the tab, paid the bills, driven me around, listened to me cry, listened to my manic ramblings. They have cooked for me, cleaned for me, encouraged me to get out of bed. They have told me I was beautiful, even when I wasn't. Their love has been a warm embrace—sometimes holding me down, sometimes lifting me up. I know that I am lucky.

CHAPTER 24

Blog post

Four years ago today, I nearly died.

Each year it gets a little easier. The first year anniversary I cried. Hell, I cried every month on the second for the first year. On the second year anniversary I cried and wrote a blog. Last year I laid in bed past noon. This year—I had champagne.

I am not happy all the time; birds do not come and eat out of my hand while I sing. Some days I wake up with bedhead. I have an ugly bruise on my arm. There is a blemish on my forehead. My diet is for shit. This is my life. But I can't tell you, I don't have the words to express, how grateful I am to be alive. Grateful—it isn't a big enough word. Even when it is shitty, I am thankful. I am glad to be around to deal with the crap because I know that compared to the alternative, to death, it is a pretty sweet deal.

So tomorrow, or, on the West Coast, tonight, have a drink and toast life, because it is a precarious thing. There are no guarantees. And no matter how much it might suck at times, it is better than the alternative.

Anything Is Possible

I don't remember everything that happened the day I tried to kill myself.

I went to work. I came home. I watched the 2008 vice presidential debate with my new roommate on her laptop with a tumbler of wine in my hand. That evening I talked to my cousin quite happily on the phone with my feet dangling into the luminous pool. Had a couple cigarettes. And then I decided to die.

Sometimes when I hear sirens I cry. I think I must remember being in an ambulance, being rushed to the emergency room, even though I was unconscious. I can't explain it. I can't explain any of it.

I don't remember the doctors pumping my stomach to get out all the Xanax I had put in it. I don't remember them shoving a tube down my throat and into my lung to keep me alive. I remember waking up and my sister sitting next to the bed. It was her birthday.

I was confused and sedated. I used my rusty skills at charades to ask for a pen and some paper. I asked her to take a picture of me, as if I wouldn't remember being in the intensive care unit—much of it I don't. I keep that picture on my computer in a folder I named "bipolar." If you want to see what bipolar looks like, I can show you. It looks like cuff restraints on my wrists. A myriad of tubes coming across the bed and over my shoulder and taped into my mouth. It is a screen showing my heartbeat and blood pressure. It is a baby blue blanket and a hospital gown so big it has fallen off my shoulder. Tan skin. White and blue linens. I look small and confused. I gaze out of unseeing eyes, as though my glasses aren't really on, like I can hear, but not see, my sister.

I don't look at the picture often. I can't. I keep it to remind me of where I have been, to remind me that anything is possible. I cannot trust my mind. From that day on, I do not trust myself. Oh, I am wiser now. I can sense when my brain is threatening to leave me. I can feel a buzz, like the top of my head is coming off. It is effervescent. Sometimes I jump around and am deliriously happy and agitated. Or maybe I sleep past noon. I don't eat. I think about guns and knives and pills. Anything is possible.

I don't remember everything that happened the day I tried

to kill myself. I wrote a note. I wrote a note and all I can picture is the mattress on the floor in my new apartment where I bent over white, lined paper. I think I told my sister I was sorry. I imagine I wrote something to my mother. The words are lost like sleep is lost when your daughter tries to kill herself.

It is hard to imagine—not knowing you are going to try to commit suicide. Waking up oblivious. Going about your day. Making friends. Enjoying life. Then night falls. Then it's over.

I'd be lying if I said I never thought about killing myself again after that. I have bipolar disorder and that is perhaps the biggest lie I could tell. I have thought about it often. My will is written. My funeral music playlist is aptly called "The End." But I don't think about it today. Those days are tucked neatly behind me. Today I worry about the future. I want to get married. I want to make my parents proud. I want to meet my brother's unborn children. I want to live long enough that my sister forgives me.

October 2nd, 2007. That is the day I nearly lost my life. If I lived alone, I would be dead. If my roommate hadn't gone to the kitchen for a glass of water and found me lying unconscious on the linoleum floor, I would be dead. If she hadn't found the note I wrote while I downed fistfuls of pills, I would be dead. Death is that simple.

Here I am, four years later. And I am thankful for October 2nd, 2007, because without it I wouldn't know the love I do. I have been encouraged and supported and loved in a way I don't think I was willing to accept before. I know that I am good enough, even at my worst, that I am worthy of love and respect and gentleness and caring. I have a compassion for myself that I never had before. I know that it is okay to fail, to bow out, to simply not be up to it. I know what it means to live and to love. And I know how it feels to thank God every night for one more day because I almost wasn't here. Death is that simple.

I have overdosed more than once. I have slit my wrist so badly I have needed stitches three times. I know how precarious life is. And though there may be bad days and mania and depression and hiccups and bumps, I want to live. I want to live. I know that no matter what happens there are people who love me and will take care of me when I can't. I trust in them. They are my hope.

I took a walk yesterday on a gorgeous fall day. The air was light and there were a few leaves that had already made their voyage from lofty heights down to my feet. I smiled as the sunlight hit my face and I thought, How far I have come. Since that day that changed my life, so much has happened. I have moved four times, making my way from one coast to the other. I have seen my two best friends give birth to healthy babies. I have attended graduate school. I have fallen in love with someone who cares about me in a way no other man ever has. I have seen my sister marry. I have been hospitalized three times, but it has been over a year and a half since I last saw the inside of an emergency room. I am stronger now. I am braver now.

Today I am happy. Tomorrow may be different. I know now that even if the darkness comes, so, too, will the light. It isn't an easy way to live, never knowing who I am going to be from one hour to the next. My moods are like a summer thunderstorm— unpredictable and charged. But I am more stable today than I have been in years. I try not to cut. I don't throw up. I don't take too many pills. Instead, I write. I say things the only way I know how. I chain words together to form sentences. I lasso sentences around the moon.

I don't remember everything that happened the day I tried to kill myself, but I do know why I will live. I will live because tomorrow could be better than today. I have come so far and I have so much farther to go. I know that anything is possible.

ACKNOWLEDGMENTS

First and foremost, I want to thank God for this life He continues to let me lead. I thank Him for giving me the words to write this book and the patience and the dedication that comes along with a task such as this. My life is precarious and so far, He has kept me here, despite my attempts to kill myself, and for that I am thankful.

I want to thank my loving family. Angela, I know I put you through hell and I am sorry. Thanks for being there for me when you could. I hope you can forgive me and I hope we can be close again. Dad, thank you for making me feel strong and for showing a gentle compassion when I was "unwell." James, you were just cool. You designed my "Love" tattoo and every time I look at it I am reminded not only to love myself, but that others love me. You made me feel normal and that I will always treasure. Kimberly, you were there during one of the darkest times of my life and you taught me how to laugh again. I will be forever grateful for your company. Mom, you've been my rock. I would have never made it to all those appointments if it weren't for you and our customary cups of coffee. I wouldn't have remembered my meds. I wouldn't have had the courage to move out and start my life all over again. Our chats are often the highlight of my day. I know I worry you—all of you—but I am trying my best to be here and to be strong and to be hopeful.

I don't know if I'd be sitting here writing these acknowledgments if it weren't for my ex-boyfriend, Jeremy. He has supported me and this book from the beginning, allowing me a place and time to write. He helped me shrug off the rejections of agents. He came to my readings of chapters of this memoir in progress. His support finished this project.

This book wouldn't have happened if it weren't for my class-mates at The Muse in Norfolk, Virginia. They critiqued chapters, told me what wasn't working and what was. I want to especially thank my teacher, Janine Latus, from whom I learned so much and without whom this book would be so much less than it turned out to be. Also, a shout out to my classmates—Michelle Johnson, Michael Withiam, Betsy Landy Hnath, and Laura Vivi-ana. You are all so talented and I am lucky to have met you.

My first readers are very dear to me. I sent them each my manuscript with no expectations, only anticipation of their thoughts. They identified mistakes, offered suggestions, and were the best mix of women I could have chosen to read this book. Thank you, Laura Neilsen, not only for your critique and praise, but also for your brownies—both the ones as an inpa-tient in a psych ward and the ones in celebration of finishing my book. They were delicious. Thank you, Sandy Morris Mauri-ello. You are one of the most talented writers I know and even though graduate school didn't go as planned for either of us, I got you out of it. Thanks to Samantha Adams Becker, my former right-hand woman, forever friend, and gorgeous writer in her own right. Thanks to Heather Timmons for taking the time to read this beast of a project. I know how busy you are and what a sacrifice that time taken was; I will always appreciate you.

Jenna Bagnini, you are an editorial goddess. You found so many little things that the rest of us missed. You made this thing—this book, this labor of love—cleaner. Thank you for ev-ery comma addition, phrase deletion, and smart italicization.

Eric, Michelle, Brandon, and Connor Peterson are a colorful family who contributed to the making of the memoir in a large financial way. Thank you.

Thanks to Hope and Sammy, for getting me out of bed ev-ery day, for keeping me company, for not complaining when my mood turns sour, and for staying out of the kitchen when I've shattered half a dozen drinking glasses out of frustration. You two dogs are my children and I love you from your wet noses to your furry tails.

There Comes a Light

The great photography was created by Jen Wilson on the front and Sharon Martin on the back. Awesome.

Thanks to all the readers of my blogs over the years. Your heartfelt messages have meant so much to me. All I've wanted to do since I have accepted my mental illnesses is to help others feel like you weren't alone, because you're not.

You've got me.

www.ingramcontent.com/pod-product-compliance
Lightning Source LLC
Chambersburg PA
CBHW071529040426
42452CB00008B/938